J. W Dadmun

The New Melodeon

a collection of hymns and tunes, original and selected, adapted to all occasions of

social worship

J. W Dadmun

The New Melodeon
a collection of hymns and tunes, original and selected, adapted to all occasions of social worship

ISBN/EAN: 9783337291365

Printed in Europe, USA, Canada, Australia, Japan

Cover: Foto ©Thomas Meinert / pixelio.de

More available books at **www.hansebooks.com**

THE

NEW MELODEON:

A COLLECTION OF

HYMNS AND TUNES,

ORIGINAL AND SELECTED.

ADAPTED TO

All Occasions of Social Worship.

BY REV. J. W. DADMUN.

AUTHOR OF "REVIVAL MELODIES," "MELODEON," ETC.

BOSTON:
FOR SALE BY J. P. MAGEE,
NO. 5 CORNHILL.

Entered according to Act of Congress, in the year 1866, by J. W. DADMUN, in the Clerk's office of the District Court of Massachusetts.

PREFACE.

The MELODEON has been before the public for about six years, and the favor with which it has been received by the Christian churches has induced the author to publish a new book under the title of THE NEW MELODEON.

Retaining all the popular melodies of the old Melodeon, we have added over fifty pages of new music, making it the most complete book of the kind in the market. Many of the hymns, as well as the tunes, have been composed expressly for this work; and we are confident that some of the new melodies will be as popular as any we have ever published. New music adds new life to social worship, especially when it is cheerful and appropriate. "Rejoice in the Lord, O ye righteous; for praise is comely for the upright. Praise the Lord with harp, sing unto him with the psaltery and an instrument of ten strings. Sing unto him a new song; play skillfully with a loud noise."

A. B. KIDDER'S MUSIC TYPOGRAPHY.

THE NEW MELODEON.

THE TOMB IS VOID. 6s.

J. W. D.

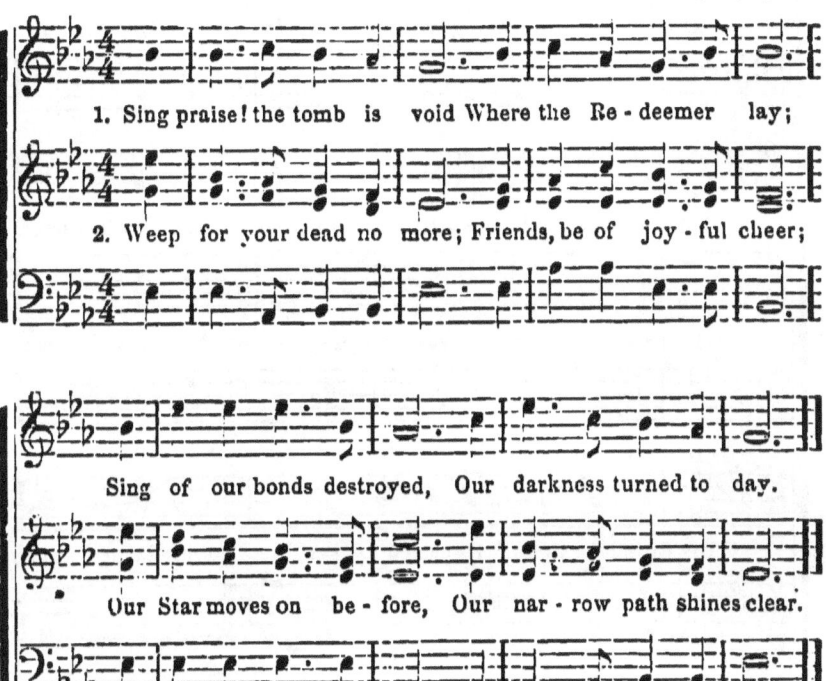

1. Sing praise! the tomb is void Where the Redeemer lay;
2. Weep for your dead no more; Friends, be of joyful cheer;

Sing of our bonds destroyed, Our darkness turned to day.
Our Star moves on before, Our narrow path shines clear.

3 He, who so patiently,
  The crown of thorns did wear,—
  He hath gone up on high;
  Our hope is with him there.

4 Now is truth revealed,
  His majesty and might;
  The grave has been unsealed;
  Christ is our life and light.

5 He who for men did weep;
  Suffer, and bleed, and die,—
  First-fruits of them that sleep,—
  Christ has gone up on high.

6 His vict'ry hath destroyed
  The shafts that once would slay;
  Sing praise! the tomb is void
  Where the Redeemer lay.

4. THE LANGUAGE OF THE CROSS. C. M.

J. W. D.

1. In evil long I took delight, Unawed by shame or fear,
Till a new object struck my sight, And stopped my wild career.

2. I saw one hanging on a tree, In ag-o-nies and blood,
Who fix'd His languid eyes on me, As near his cross I stood.

CHORUS.
"The Cross! the Cross!" it seemed to say, As on the Lamb I gazed,
"This blood is for thy ransom paid, Believe, and thou art saved."

GOD IS LOVE. L. M.

J. W. D.

1. I cannot always trace the way, Where Thou, Almighty One dost move;
But I can always, always say That God is love, that God is love.

2. When fear her chilling mantle flings O'er earth, my soul to heav'n above,
As to her sanc-tu-a-ry springs, For God is love, for God is love.

3 When myst'ry clouds my darkened path,
I'll check my dread, my doubts reprove;
In this my soul sweet comfort hath,
That God is love, that God is love.

4 Yes, God is love: — a thought like this
Can every gloomier thought remove,
And turn all tears, all woes to bliss—
For God is love, for God is love.

Conclusion of hymn on opposite page.

3 Sure never till my latest breath,
   Can I forget that look;
It seemed to charge me with his death,
   Though not a word he spoke.

4 My conscience felt and owned the guilt,
   And plunged me in despair;
I saw my sins his blood had spilt,
   And helped to nail him there.

5 Alas! I knew not what I did:
   But now my tears are vain;
Where shall my trembling soul be hid?
   For I the Lord have slain.

6 A second look he gave, which said,
   "I freely all forgive;
This blood is for thy ransom paid,
   I die that thou may'st live."

THE WANDERER RECALLED. L. M.

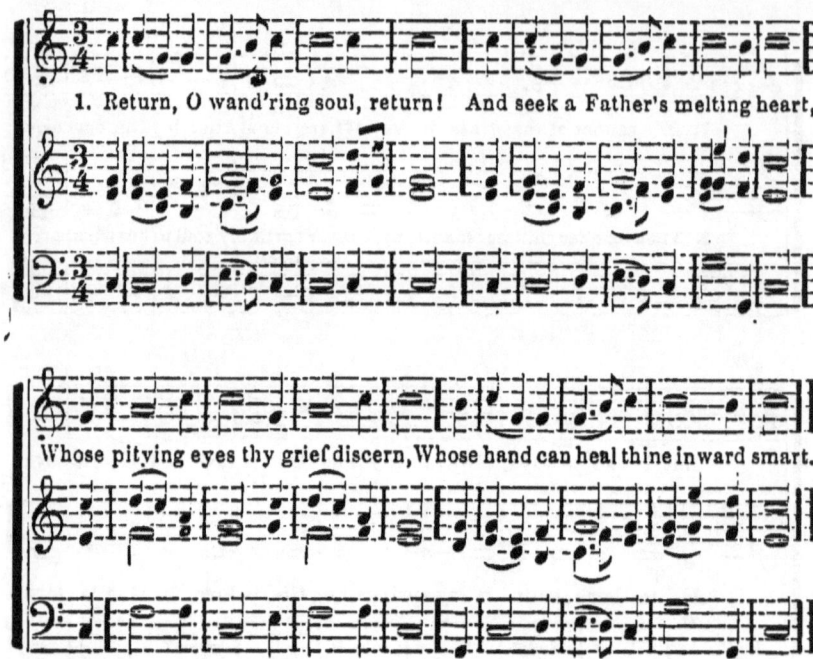

1. Return, O wand'ring soul, return! And seek a Father's melting heart, Whose pitying eyes thy grief discern, Whose hand can heal thine inward smart.

2 Return, O wand'ring soul, return!
　He heard thy deep repentant sigh;
He saw thy softened spirit mourn,
　When no intruding tear was nigh.

3 Return, O wand'ring soul, return!
　Thy dying Saviour bids thee live;
Go to his bleeding side, and learn
　How freely Jesus can forgive.

4 Return, O wand'ring soul, return!
　Come, wipe away the flowing tear;
'Tis God who says—"no longer mourn,"
　'Tis mercy's voice invites thee near.

5 Return, O wand'ring soul, return!
　Regain thy long-forsaken rest:
The Saviour's melting mercies yearn
　To clasp thee to his loving breast.

Stay, insulted Spirit. L. M.

1 Stay, thou insulted Spirit, stay,
　Tho' I have done thee such despite;
Nor cast the sinner quite away,
　Nor take thine everlasting flight.

2 Tho' I have steel'd my stubborn heart,
　And shaken off my guilty fears;
And vex'd, and urged thee to depart,
　For many long rebellious years;

3 Though I have most unfaithful been,
　Of all who e'er thy grace received;
Ten thousand times thy goodness seen,
Ten thousand times thy goodness grieved:

4 Yet, oh! the chief of sinners spare,
　In honor of my great High Priest;
Nor in thy righteous anger swear
　To exclude me from thy people's rest.
　　　　　　　　　　　C WESLEY.

JESUS CALLS YOU. P. M.

J. W. D.

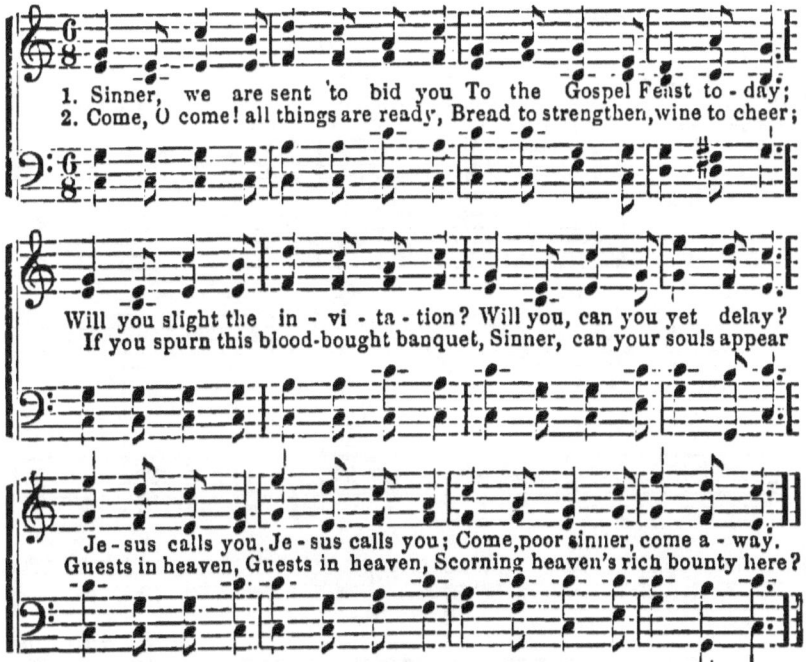

1. Sinner, we are sent to bid you To the Gospel Feast to-day;
Will you slight the in-vi-ta-tion? Will you, can you yet delay?
Je-sus calls you, Je-sus calls you; Come, poor sinner, come a-way.

2. Come, O come! all things are ready, Bread to strengthen, wine to cheer;
If you spurn this blood-bought banquet, Sinner, can your souls appear
Guests in heaven, Guests in heaven, Scorning heaven's rich bounty here?

3 Come, O come! leave father, mother;
  To your Saviour's bosom fly:
Leave the worthless world behind you,
  Seek for pardon, or you die:
    "Pardon, Saviour!"
Hear the sinking sinner cry.

4 Even now the Holy Spirit
  Moves upon some melting heart,
Pleads a bleeding Saviour's merit;
  Sinner, will you say, "Depart?"
    Wretched sinner,
Can you bid your God depart?

5 What are all earth's dearest pleasures,
  Were they more than tongue can tell?
What are all its boasted treasures
  To a soul when sunk in hell?
    Treasure! pleasure!
No such sounds are heard in hell.

6 Fly, O! fly ye to the mountain,
  Linger not in all the plain;
Leave this Sodom of corruption,
  Turn not, look not back again:
    Fly to Jesus,
Linger not in all the plain!

LAKE ENON. S. M.

I. B. WOODBURY. By permission.

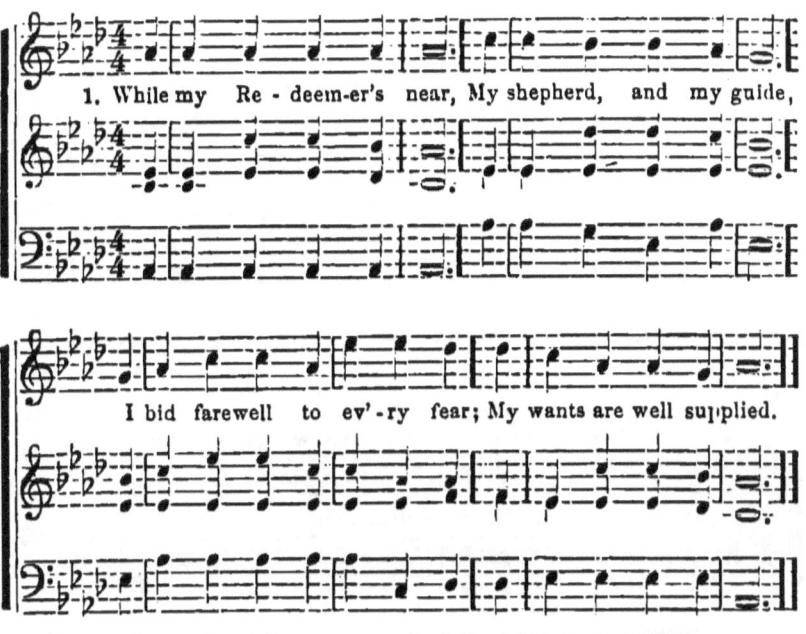

1. While my Re-deem-er's near, My shepherd, and my guide, I bid farewell to ev'-ry fear; My wants are well supplied.

2 To ever fragrant meads,
Where rich abundance grows,
His gracious hand indulgent leads,
And guards my sweet repose.

3 Dear Shepherd, if I stray,
My wandering feet restore:
And guard me with thy watchful eye
And let me rove no more.

Conclusion of hymn on opposite page.

2 They have come so near that I hear them sing,
  And they bid me be brave and strong,
Though the water's cold, and the way seems dark,
  Yet the struggle will not be long.

3 I can hear them sing, and they know I come
  With no fear of the cold dark wave;
And my faith is strong that I yet shall *shout*,
  For where is thy sting, oh! grave?

4 Full many times I have watched with pain,
  As the loved of my heart went away;
But I know they're safe in our Father's home,
  And are waiting for me, to-day.

5 I am coming, dear ones, my steps are slow,
  For the cross is so heavy to bear;—
Though my wings are spread, yet I cannot fly,
  Like the bird from the fowler's snare.

SAINT'S CORONATION DAY. L. M.

Music by Rev. L. Hartsough.

1. Sweet day of rest, sweet day of rest! I long to see thee and be blest;
D.C. The weary saint will then be blest, When thou shalt come, sweet day of rest;

I long to know thy peaceful light, And wear the robe of spotless white.
The weary saint will then be blest, When thou shalt come, sweet day of rest

When Jesus comes on earth to reign, The wilderness shall bloom a-gain.

2 Sweet promis'd land, sweet promis'd land!
By faith I view thee near at hand;
O may my anxious spirit burn
With warm desires for thy return;
With joy I read thy blessed word,
That hope shall not be long deferred,
And gladly join the pilgrim band
That long for thee, sweet promis'd land.

3 Lord Jesus, come, Lord Jesus come,
And take thy waiting people home!
Let earth her sleeping jewels yield;
Let Satan vanquished quit the field;
O may we soon behold our King,
And shout, O death where is thy sting!
Lord Jesus, come, Lord Jesus, come,
And take us to our promised home.

Conclusion of hymn on opposite page.

3 Softly thus they hedge my wand'rings,
. And would save me from the snare;
Sweetly would they lead to Jesus,
When I wander here and there.

4 Lord I praise Thee! Thou hast sent them
Thus to guard with gentle care;
May I live so that in dying
They, my soul above may bear.

SERAPHIC FIRE. 8 lines, 7s.

J. W. D.

1. Light of life,—se-raph-ic fire, Love di-vine, thyself im-part:
Eve-ry fainting soul in-spire; Shine in eve-ry drooping heart.
Son of God! appear! appear! To thy human temples come.

Eve-ry mournful sin-ner cheer; Scatter all our guilt-y gloom,

For reviving grace.

2 Come in this accepted hour,
  Bring thy heavenly kingdom in;
Fill us with thy glorious power,
  Rooting out the seeds of sin;
Nothing more can we require,
  We will count nothing less;
Be thou all our heart's desire,—
  All our joy, and all our peace.

Tender expostulation.

1 Sinners turn while God is near;
  Dare not think him insincere;
Now, even now, your Saviour stands,
  All day long he spreads his hands;
Cries,—" ye will not happy be;
  No, ye will not come to me,—
Me, who life to none deny;
  Why will ye resolve to die?"

2 Turn, he cries, ye sinners, turn;
  By his life your God hath sworn;
He would have you turn and live,
  He would all the world receive;
If your death were his delight,
  Would he you to life invite?
Would he ask, beseech, and cry,—
  Why will ye resolve to die?

3 What could your Redeemer do,
  More than he hath done for you?
To procure your peace with God,
  Could he more than shed his blood?
After all his flow of love,
  All his drawings from above,—
Why will ye your Lord deny?
  Why will ye resolve to die?

CLEANSING FOUNTAIN. C. M.

Furnished by MRS. REV. F. BOTTOME.

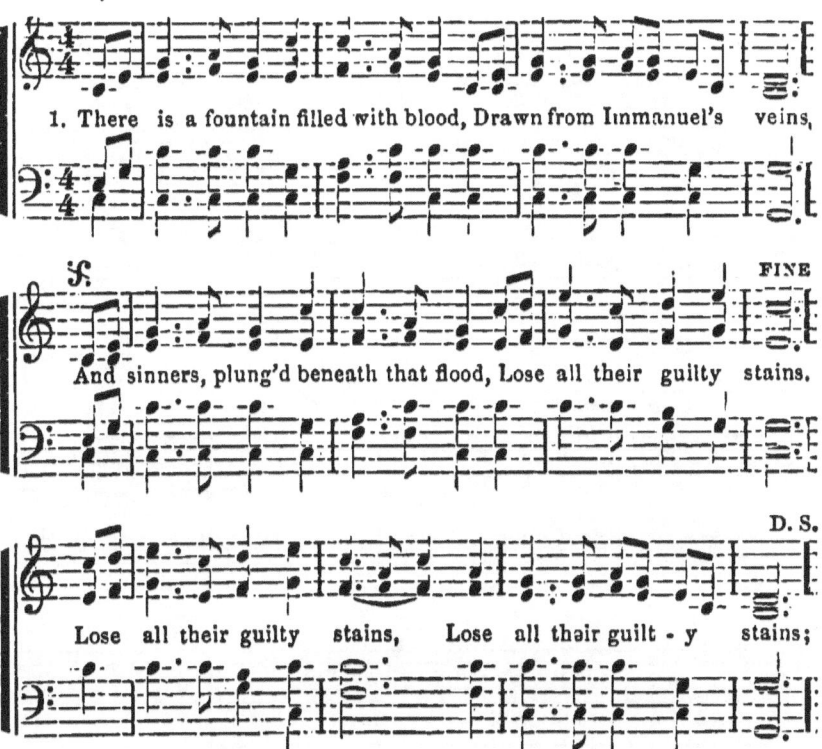

1. There is a fountain filled with blood, Drawn from Immanuel's veins, And sinners, plung'd beneath that flood, Lose all their guilty stains. Lose all their guilty stains, Lose all their guilt-y stains;

2 The dying thief rejoiced to see
That fountain in his day;
And there may I, though vile as he
Wash all my sins away.

3 Thou dying Lamb! thy precious blood
Shall never lose its power,
'Till all the ransom'd Church of God
Are saved, to sin no more.

4 E'er since by faith I saw the stream
Thy flowing wounds supply,
Redeeming love has been my theme,
And shall be, till I die.

5 Then in a nobler, sweeter song,
I'll sing thy power to save,
When this poor lisping, stamm'ring tongue
Lies silent in the grave

THE RESOLUTION. C. M.

1 Come, humble sinner, in whose breast
A thousand thoughts revolve;
Come, with your guilt and fear oppress'd
And make this last resolve:

2 I'll go to Jesus, though my sin
Like mountains round me close;
I know his courts, I'll enter in,
Whatever may oppose.

3 Prostrate I'll lie before his throne,
And there my guilt confess;
I'll tell him I'm a wretch undone,
Without his sovereign grace.

4 I can but perish if I go,
I am resolved to try;
For if I stay away I know
I must forever die.

PLEYEL'S HYMN. 7s.

1. Softly fades the twilight ray Of the holy Sabbath day;
2. Night her solemn mantle spreads O'er the earth, as daylight fades;
Gently as life's setting sun, When the Christian's course is run.
All things tell of calm repose, At the holy Sabbath's close.

Sabbath Evening.

3 Peace is on the world abroad;
'Tis the holy peace of God,—
Symbol of the peace within,
When the spirit rests from sin.

4 Saviour, may our Sabbaths be
Days of peace and joy in thee,
Till in heaven our souls repose,
Where the Sabbath ne'er shall close.

Conclusion of hymn on opposite page.

2 And when I was willing with all things to part,
He gave me my bounty, his love in my heart;
So now I am joined with the conquering band,
Who are marching to glory at Jesus' command.

3 Though round me the storms of adversity roll,
And the waves of destruction encompass my soul,
In vain this frail vessel the tempest shall toss,
My hopes rest secure on the blood of the cross.

4 And when the last trumpet of judgment shall sound,
And wake all the nations that sleep in the ground,
Then, when heaven and earth shall be melting away,
I'll sing of the blood of the cross in that day.

5 And when with the ransomed by Jesus, my head,
From fountain to fountain I then shall be led;
I'll fall at his feet, and his mercy adore,
And sing of the blood of the cross evermore.

HE IS PRECIOUS. 7s & 6s.

J. W. D.

1. My soul is now u-nit-ed To Christ, the liv-ing vine;
2. I was to God a stranger, Till Je-sus took me in,

His grace I long have slighted, But now I feel him mine.
And freed my soul from dan-ger, And pardoned all my sin.

CHORUS.

Christ is all the world to me; And his glo-ry I shall see,

And be-fore I'd leave my Saviour, I'd lay me down to die.

LIGHT IS BREAKING. 8s & 7s. 17

Arranged.

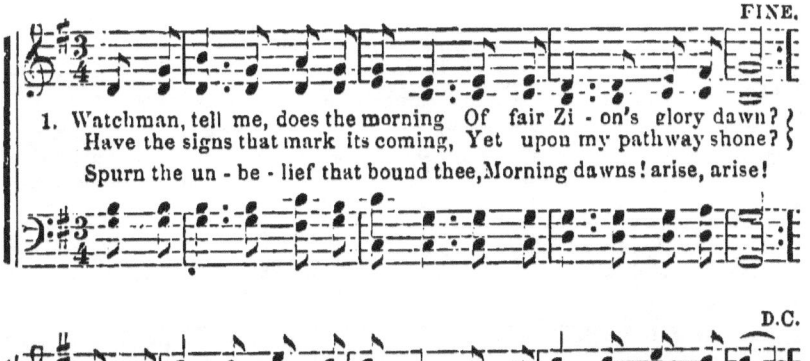

1. Watchman, tell me, does the morning Of fair Zi-on's glory dawn?
Have the signs that mark its coming, Yet upon my pathway shone?
Spurn the un-be-lief that bound thee, Morning dawns! arise, arise!

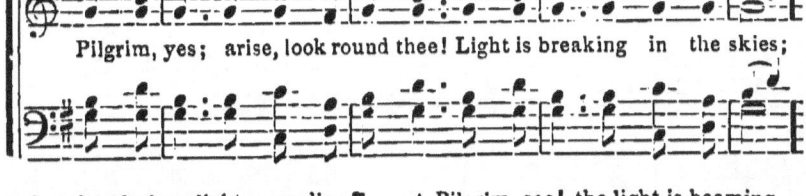

Pilgrim, yes; arise, look round thee! Light is breaking in the skies;

2 See the glorious light ascending,
 Of the grand Sabbatic year!
Hark! the voices loud proclaiming
 The Messiah's kingdom near.
Watchman! yes; I see just yonder,
 Canaan's glorious heights arise;
Salem, too, appears in grandeur,
 Towering 'neath her sunlit skies.

3 Pilgrim, in that golden city,
 Seated on his jasper throne,
Zion's King, arrayed in beauty,
 Reigns in peace from zone to zone;
There, on verdant hills and mountains,
 Where the golden sunbeams play,
Purling streams and crystal fountains,
 Sparkle in th' eternal day.

4 Pilgrim, see! the light is beaming
 Brighter still upon thy way;
Signs thro' all the earth are gleaming,
 Omens of thy coming day.
When the last loud trumpet sounding,
 Shall awake, from earth and sea,
All the saints of God now sleeping,
 Clad in immortality.

5 Watchman, lo! the land we're nearing,
 With its vernal fruits and flow'rs;
On just yonder, O how cheering!
 Bloom forever Eden's bowers.
Hark! the choral strains there ringing,
 Wafted on the balmy air;
See the millions: hear them singing,
 Soon the pilgrims will be there.

Conclusion of hymn on opposite page.

3 Soon as my all I ventured
 On the atoning blood,
His Holy Spirit entered,
 And I was born of God.

4 Still Christ is my Salvation;
 What can I covet more?
I fear no condemnation;
 My Father's wrath is o'er.

5 By floods and flames surrounded,
 I now my way pursue;
Nor shall I be confounded
 With glory in my view.

6 I taste a heavenly pleasure,
 And need not fear a frown;
Christ is my joy and treasure,
 My glory and my crown.

[2]

HEAVEN'S NOT FAR AWAY. C. M.

Words by MABELLE.
J. W. D.

1. I'm ve-ry near my Father's house, Its jasper walls I see;
The pearly gates are o-pen wide, But can it be for me?
I see the blest an-gel-ic throng, But yet they seem to wait,
For leave to spread their folded wings, And pass beyond the gate.

O, WHERE SHALL REST BE FOUND? S. M. 19

S. HILL.

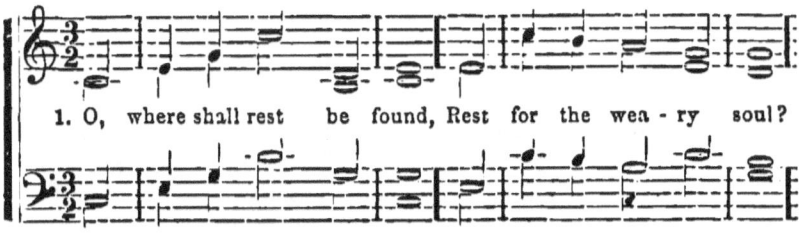

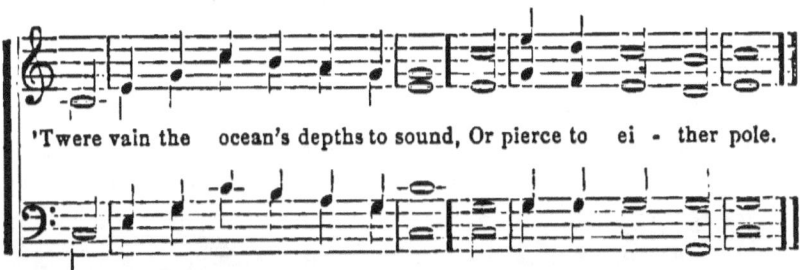

2 The world can never give
  The bliss for which we sigh;
  'Tis not the whole of life to live,
  Nor all of death to die.

3 Beyond this vale of tears
  There is a life above,
  Unmeasured by the flight of years,
  And all that life is love.

4 There is a death, whose pang
  Outlasts the fleeting breath;
  O what eternal horrors hang
  Around the second death!

5 Thou God of truth and grace!
  Teach us that death to shun;
  Lest we be banished from thy face,
  Forever more undone.

Conclusion of hymn on opposite page.

2 I see a bright and starry crown,
  Which one is holding now;
  As if her heavenly mission was,
  To crown some saintly brow.
  I see a harp with strings all tuned,—
  I wait to catch its sound;
  But in the City of our God,
  No empty hand is found.

3 I see a robe of glorious form,
  On which no stain is seen;
  And all God's children now are cloth'd
  In such a saintly sheen.

I see it there in angel hands,
  With crown and harp of gold;
  The waiting soul is still on earth,
  To pass death's waters cold.

4 I see the Saviour's crown of thorns,
  Which once He wore for me;
  And now, my earnest cry is, Lord,
  What can I do for Thee?
  More than to take my heavy cross,
  And wait thy will to know;—
  For till I'm needed in thy courts,—
  I would not *want* to go!

SALVATION. C. M.

H. W. BOWEN.

3 Salvation! let the echo fly
　The spacious earth around,
While all the armies of the sky
　Conspire to raise the sound.

4 Salvation! O, thou bleeding Lamb,
　To thee the praise belongs;
Salvation shall inspire our hearts,
　And dwell upon our tongues.

GOD IS NEAR THEE. 6s & 5s.

Words and Music by REV. L. HARTSOUGH.

1. Listen to the whisp'rings Of the Spirit near, Calling to sal-vation, And from sin and fear; By them you may gather Light, and life and power.

CHORUS.
Freedom from the lurings Of temptation's hour. God is near thee night and day; God will hear thee, therefore pray, God is near thee night and day; God will hear thee, (OMIT.........) therefore pray.

2 Listen to the pleadings
      Of the Saviour's love;
   Calling thee from sinning,
      To His home above.
   He will save from sorrow,
      And the night of death;
   And the dread hereafter
      Where is felt his wrath.

3 He is fitting mansions
      For His followers true;
   There is room now waiting,
      Waiting just for you.

   Will you taste the raptures,
      That His saints shall know?
   Will you love the Saviour
      And to glory go?

4 Come then to the fountain,
      Gushing from his side;
   God and Heaven invite you,
      Plunge beneath the tide;
   There is peace and pardon
      For each sin-sick soul,
   Hallelujah, glory!
      Jesus died for all.

SHALL WE KNOW EACH OTHER THERE?

J. W. D.

1. When we hear the music ringing Thro' the bright celestial dome, When sweet angel voices ringing, Gladly bid us welcome home, To the land of ancient story, Where the spirit knows no care; In that land of light and glory, "Shall we know each other there?"

2 When the holy angels meet us,
   As we go to join this band,
Shall we know the friends that greet us
   In the glorious spirit land?
Shall we see their bright eyes shining
   On us as in days of yore?
Shall we feel their dear arms twining
   Fondly round us as before?

3 Yes, my earth-worn soul rejoices,
   And my weary heart grows light,
For the thrilling angel-voices,
   And the angel-faces bright,
That shall welcome us in heaven,
   Are the loved of long ago,
And to them 'tis kindly given
   Thus their mortal friends to know.

4 O! ye weary ones, and tost ones,
   Droop not, faint not by the way;
Ye shall join the loved and lost ones
   In the land of perfect day.
Harp-strings touched by angel-fingers
   Murmur in my raptured ear;
Ever more their sweet tone lingers,
   "We shall know each other there."

THERE, THERE IS REST. P. M.

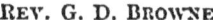

REV. G. D. BROWNE.

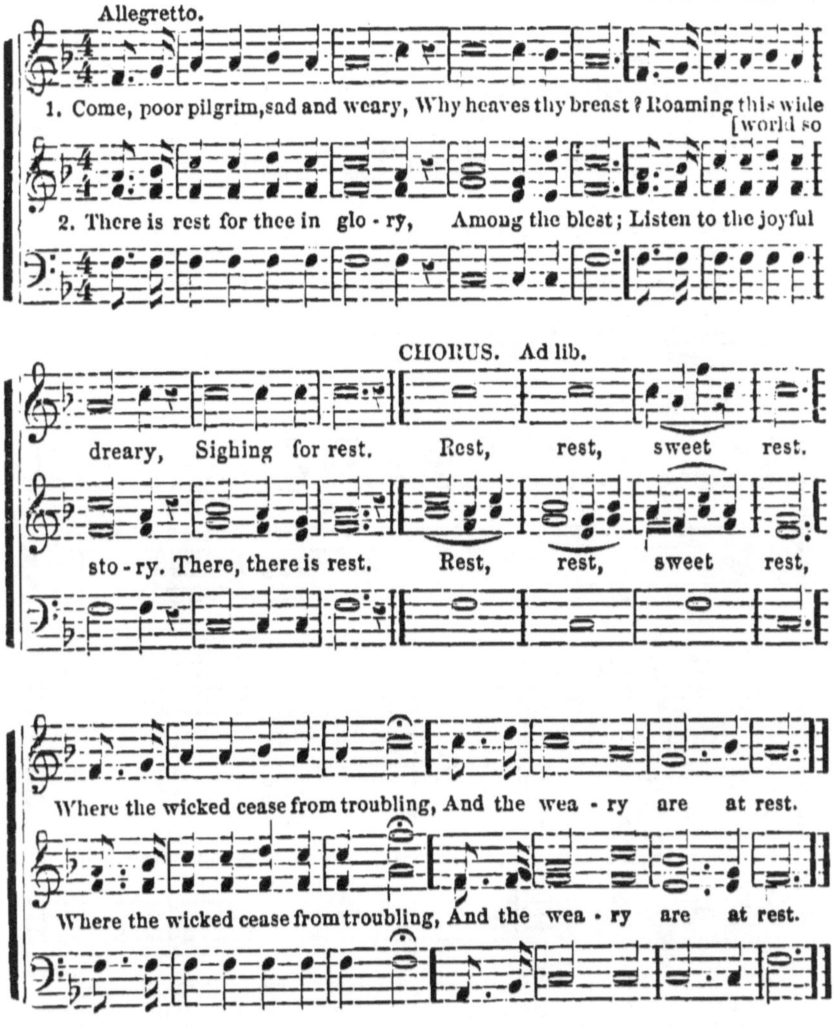
Allegretto.
1. Come, poor pilgrim, sad and weary, Why heaves thy breast? Roaming this wide [world so
2. There is rest for thee in glo - ry, Among the blest; Listen to the joyful
CHORUS. Ad lib.
dreary, Sighing for rest. Rest, rest, sweet rest.
sto - ry. There, there is rest. Rest, rest, sweet rest,
Where the wicked cease from troubling, And the wea - ry are at rest.
Where the wicked cease from troubling, And the wea - ry are at rest.

3 There are those who've gone before us,
All who are blest,
Singing now the happy chorus,
There, there is rest.

4 There the golden harps are ringing,
Harps of the blest;
And the angel bands are singing,
There, there is rest.

5 And while we on earth are praying,
Jesus, the blest,
Unto us is sweetly saying,
There, there is rest.

6 We shall meet where parting never
Comes to the blest;
And we'll safely dwell forever,
In heavenly rest

3 Sweet to look back and see my name
   In life's fair book set down;
   Sweet to look forward, and behold
   Eternal joys my own;—

4 Sweet to reflect how grace divine
   My sins on Jesus laid;
   Sweet to remember that his blood
   My debt of suff'ring paid;—

5 Sweet to rejoice in lively hope,
   That, when my change shall come,
   Angels shall hover round my bed,
   And waft my spirit home.

6 If such the sweetness of the stream,
   What must the fountain be,
   Where saints and angels draw their bliss
   Directly, Lord, from thee?

WHO CAN TELL?

J. W. D.

1. The flowery field of youth she trod, On which her eyes delighted fell, The Saviour called: 'Forsake thy toys!' She would not listen to his voice—And who can tell? O, who can tell?

2 The spring-time quickly passed away
From off the hill-side and the dell;
And then, we saw her pressed with cares,
Unmindful of her soul's affairs—
   And, who can tell? &c.

3 When on her dying bed she lay,
She dreamed she heard the fun'ral knell,
"A little longer!" then she cried,
"A year! a day!" and so she died—
   Ah!—who can tell? &c.

4 Fain would we hope when o'er the grave
Her spirit hovered, all was well.
That, at the last, the Saviour smiled,
And owned the sufferer as his child,
   But, who can tell? &c.

5 Then, seek the Saviour in thy youth,
Early, thy sinful passions quell;
Now, for the better world prepare,
For death may come ere you're aware,
   And—who can tell? &c.

H. REED.

WILLIE'S GONE BEFORE. C. M.

Words by MRS. P. A. HANAFORD.* J. W. D.

1. He's gone to that fair land of light, Where lit-tle children dwell,
Where ho-ly bliss hath no al-loy, And sin weaves no dark spell.

2. He rests with those who've run the race, And won the victor's crown,
With Christ-like souls of eve-ry age, Who've gained the saint's renown.

CHORUS.
Oh yes, we know our dar-ling Has on-ly gone be-fore;
He is singing with the an-gels, Up-on the radiant shore.

3 He'll be among the shining host,
   To greet us when we land;
Where many long departed friends
   Hath touched the glorious strand.

4 We'll clasp him to our breasts again;
   Our precious, angel boy!
And bless the love that early took
   Him to that world of joy.

* "Respectfully inscribed to REV. MR. & MRS. DADMUN, on the departure of their little son, WILLIAM ELLSWORTH."

ALAS! AND DID MY SAVIOUR BLEED. C. M. 27

From "ATHENÆUM COLLECTION," by permission. S. J. VAIL.

1. A-las! and did my Saviour bleed? And did my Sovereign die?
D.C. Yes, Je-sus died for all mankind, Bless God, he died for me.

Would he devote that sacred head For such a worm as I?

CHORUS. Je-sus died for you, Je-sus died for me;

2 Was it for crimes that I had done
   He groaned upon the tree?
   Amazing pity! grace unknown!
   And love beyond degree!

3 Well might the sun in darkness hide,
   And shut his glories in,
   When Christ the mighty Maker, died
   For man the creature's sin.

4 Thus might I hide my blushing face,
   While his dear cross appears;
   Dissolve my heart in thankfulness,
   And melt mine eyes to tears.

5 But drops of grief can ne'er repay
   The debt of love I owe:
   Here, Lord, I give myself away;
   'Tis all that I can do.

REST. C. M.

1 I saw one hanging on a tree,
   In agonies and blood,
   Who fix'd His languid eyes on me,
   As near his cross I stood.

2 Sure never till my latest breath,
   Can I forget that look;
   It seem'd to charge me with his death,
   Though not a word he spoke.

3 My conscience felt and owned the guilt,
   And plunged me in despair;
   I saw my sins his blood had spilt,
   And helped to nail him there.

4 Alas! I knew not what I did;
   But now my tears are vain;
   Where shall my trembling soul be hid?
   For I the Lord have slain.

5 A second look he gave, which said,
   "I freely all forgive;
   This blood is for thy ransom paid,
   I die that thou may'st live."

ZION'S PILGRIM. L. M.

WM. B. BRADBURY.

1. Pilgrims, we are, to Canaan bound, Our journey lies along this road;
This wil-der-ness we travel round, To reach the city of our God.

D.C. Our robes are wash'd in Jesus' blood, And we are trav'ling home to God.

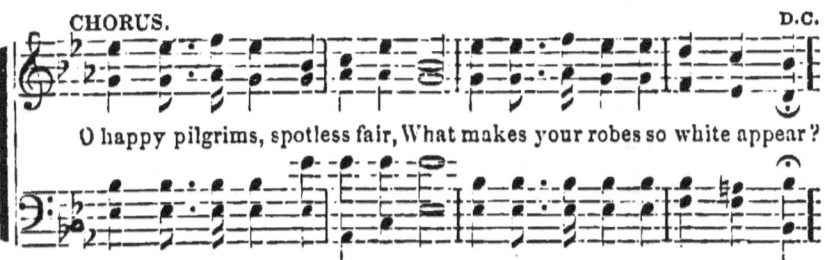

CHORUS.

O happy pilgrims, spotless fair, What makes your robes so white appear?

2 A few more days, or weeks, or years,
In this dark desert to complain;
A few more sighs, a few more tears,
And we shall bid adieu to pain.

3 O blessed land! O happy land!
When shall we reach thy golden shore,
And one redeemed, unbroken band,
United be for evermore?

4 And if our robes are pure and white,
May we all reach that blest abode?
O yes, they all shall dwell in light,
Whose robes are wash'd in Jesus' blood.

5 O may we meet at last above,
Amid the holy blood-wash'd throng;
And sing for ever Jesus' love,
While saints and angels join the song.

Conclusion of hymn on opposite page.

3 In vain thou strugglest to get free,
I never will unloose my hold;
Art thou the man that died for me?
The secret of thy love unfold;
Wrestling, I will not let thee go,
'Till I thy name, thy nature know.

4 Wilt not yet to me reveal
Thy new, unutterable name?
Tell me, I still beseech thee, tell;
To know it now resolved I am;
Wrestling, I will not let thee go,
Till I thy name, thy nature know.

5 Yield to me now, for I am weak,
But confident in self-despair,
Speak to my heart, in blessings speak;
Be conquered by my instant prayer;
Speak, or thou never hence shalt move,
And tell me if thy name is Love.

6 'Tis Love! 'tis Love! thou diedst for me;
I hear thy whisper in my heart;
The morning breaks, the shadows flee;
Pure, universal Love thou art;
To me, to all, thy bowels move,
Thy nature and thy name is Love.

HOME OF THE BLEST.

Words and Melody by J. A. HANDY. Arranged by C. H. FAXON.

Moderato.

1. In Heaven, bright Heaven, the Home of the blest, Where sorrow's unknown, I am longing to rest; To gain its fair portals my efforts shall be, For loved ones are waiting in Heaven for me,—To gain its fair portals my efforts shall be, For lov'd ones are waiting in Heaven for me.

2 To Heaven, sweet Heaven, I'm hoping to go,
When I have accomplished my mission below;
The Bible forever my standard shall be,
For loved ones are waiting in Heaven for me.

3 For Heaven I'm striving, and ne'er will give o'er,
Till safely I stand on the glittering shore;
Beyond the dark waters of life's stormy sea,
With loved ones now waiting in Heaven for me.

LET GO THE ANCHOR. 8s & 7s.

J. W. D.

1. "Land ahead!" its fruits are waving, On the hills of fadeless green; And the liv-ing waters laving Shores where heav'nly forms are seen. Eden's breezes o'er it sigh, Billows kiss its strand and die: Eden's breezes o'er it sigh, Billows kiss its strand and die.

2 Onward bark! "The cape I'm rounding,"
 See the blessed wave their hands!
Hear the harps of God resounding
 From the bright immortal bands,
Rocks and storms I'll fear no more,
When on that inviting shore.

3 "Let the anchor go,"— I'm riding
 On this calm and silvery bay;
Seaward fast the tide is gliding,
 Shores in sunlight stretch away.
Strike the colors, furl the sail!
I am safe within the vail!

I SOON SHALL SEE THE DAY. C. M.

H. W. Bowen.

3 Let cares like a wild deluge come,
Let storms of sorrow fall,—
So I but safely reach my home,
My God, my heaven, my all.

4 There I shall bathe my weary soul
In seas of heavenly rest,
And not a wave of trouble roll
Across my peaceful breast.

A BEAUTIFUL HOME FOR THEE, MOTHER.

J. W. D.

Tenderly

1. There's a beau-ti-ful home for thee, mother, A home, a home for thee; In that land of bliss, where pleasure is, There, mother's, a home for thee.

CHORUS.

A beau-ti-ful home for thee, A beau-ti-ful home for thee; In that land of bliss, where pleasure is, There, mother's, a home for thee.

2 There's a beautiful rest * for thee, mother,
A rest, a rest for thee;
In that home above, where all is love,
There, mother's, a rest for thee.

3 There's a beautiful crown for thee, mother,
A beautiful crown for thee;
When the battle's fought, the vict'ry won,
Our Saviour will give it thee.

4 There's a beautiful robe for thee, mother,
A robe, a robe for thee;
A robe of white, so pure and bright,
There, mother's a robe for thee.

5 We'll seek that beautiful home, mother,
That home, that home above;
In that land of light, where all is bright,
That mansion where all is love.

* Substitute REST in the chorus.

[3]   * The CHORUS on Page 32 may be used as a Short Metre Tune.

IMMANUEL'S BIRTH, Concluded.

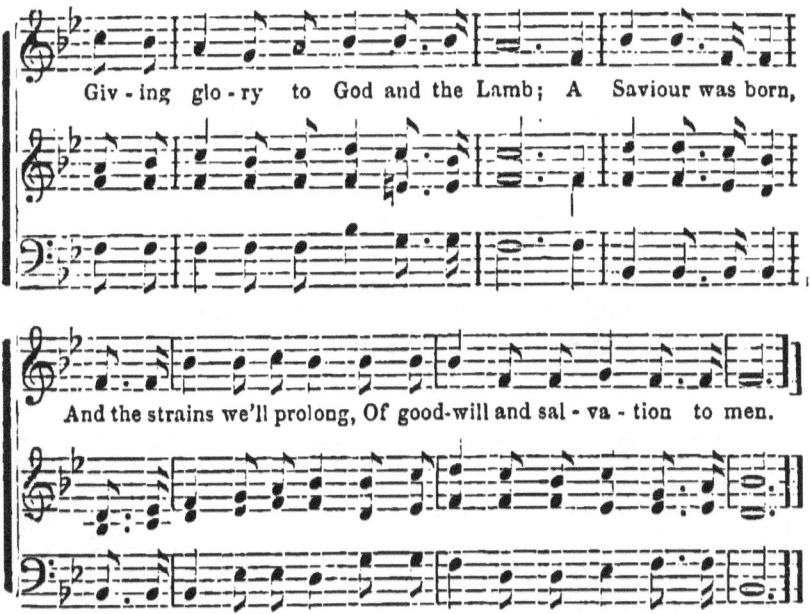

Giv-ing glo-ry to God and the Lamb; A Saviour was born,

And the strains we'll prolong, Of good-will and sal-va-tion to men.

3 O may the return
Of this once blessed morn,
Be forever remembered with joy;
Sweet accents of praise.
All our voices shall raise;
Hallelujah shall be our employ!

4 Let echo prolong
The harmonious song—
Hallelujahs again and again:
He kindles the fire,
Whom the nations desire,
And to him we devote the glad strain.

Joy of the young Convert.

1 O how happy are they,
Who the Saviour obey,
And have laid up their treasure above!
Tongue can never express
The sweet comfort and peace
Of a soul in its earliest love.

2 That sweet comfort was mine,
When the favor divine
I received thro' the blood of the Lamb;
When my heart first believed,
What a joy I received—
What a heaven in Jesus's name!

3 'Twas a heaven below
My Redeemer to know,
And the angels could do nothing more,
Than to fall at his feet,
And the story repeat,
And the Lover of sinners adore.

4 Jesus all the day long
Was my joy and my song:
Oh that all his salvation might see!
He hath loved me, I cried,
He hath suffered and died,
To redeem even rebels like me.

5 Oh, the rapturous height
Of that holy delight
Which I felt in the life-giving blood!
Of my Saviour possess'd,
I was perfectly blest,
As if fill'd with the fulness of God.

C. WESLEY.

REPENTANCE.

Words by Mrs. H. E. Brown.   Music by Mr. J. L. Ensign.

1. Blessed Jesus, when I see All thy tender care for me, All thy grace and beauty; While my heart in sin astray, Wanders from thee day by day, Far from love and duty; Pain and grief my soul oppress; I am filled with deep distress: Pain and grief my soul oppress; I am filled with deep distress.

2 I have grieved thee, well I know,
  Caused thy tears and blood to flow,
    O my suffering Saviour!
  Yet amid thy agony,
  Thou hast kindly welcomed me
    To receive thy favor!
  Oh! divinest, matchless grace!
  Even while I wound to bless!

3 Bid my tears break forth and flow,
  Bid my heart relent and bow,
    At thy feet, dear Jesus;
  Bid my voice awake and sing,
  Bid my life its tribute bring,
    All it has most precious:
  But forbid me e'er again,
  By one sin to give thee pain.

ANGELS ROUND ME. 8s & 7s.

Words and Music by REV. L. HARTSOUGH.

1. There are angels hov'ring round me; Yes, I feel them sweetly near;
2. 'Mid my toils the waiting angels Cheer me with their gladsome love,

Soon they'll bear me o'er the riv-er, Where is nev-er known a fear.
Lighting up earth's gloom and sorrow, Luring me to joys a-bove.

CHORUS.

Hasten angel bands, to bear me To the sunlight 'cross the tide.
'Mid the splendor of the mansions Where my Saviour doth a-bide.

3 Yes, there's sunlight cross the River,
  Cloudless skies are ever there;
Night will never dim the brightness,
  Of those realms of glory rare.

4 My poor body fast is sinking
  To the darkness of the tomb,
But my spirit waits the summons,
  That will upward bid it come.

5 O'er the River, not long waiting,
  Soul with body shall unite,
Never more to know corruption,
  But, like Jesus, changed and bright.

6 So I toil on,— Angels round me
  Winning me where toils come not:
I am drawing nigh the River,
  Where life's sorrows are forgot.

MERCY'S FREE. P. M. (New.)

J. W. D.

EVENING. 7s.

B. TEMPLE GEORGE.

Conclusion of hymn on opposite page.

3 Jesus, the mighty God, hath spoken
  Peace to me, peace to me;
  Now all my chains of sin are broken,
  I am free, I am free.
  Soon as I in his name believed,
  The Holy Spirit I received;
  And Christ from death my soul reprieved;
  Mercy's free, mercy's free.

4 Jesus my weary soul refreshes—
  Mercy's free, mercy's free—
  And every moment Christ is precious
  Unto me, unto me.
  None can describe the bliss I prove,
  While through this wilderness I rove;
  All may enjoy the Saviour's love—
  Mercy's free, mercy's free.

5 This precious truth, ye sinners, hear it,
  Mercy's free, mercy's free—
  Ye ministers of God, declare it—
  Mercy's free, mercy's free.
  Visit the heathen's dark abode,
  Proclaim to all the love of God,
  And spread the glorious news abroad—
  Mercy's free, mercy's free.

6 Long as I live I'll still be crying,
  Mercy's free, mercy's free;
  And this shall be my theme when dying,
  Mercy's free, mercy's free;
  And when the vale of death I've passed,
  When lodged above the stormy blast,
  I'll sing, while endless ages last,
  Mercy's free, mercy's free.

O! I WANT TO CROSS OVER!

Words and Music by REV. L. HARTSOUGH.

1. O have you not heard of that realm of delight, To which the blessed Saviour doth each one invite; 'Tis prepared for the good and the pure and the blessed; 'Tis over the River where the weary find rest.

2. Tho' death's foaming billows are rolling between, Yet glories are there such as eye hath not seen; And songs are there sung such as ear hath not caught; And the way o'er the River the Saviour hath taught.

CHORUS.—O I want to cross over, to dwell where he reigns, And join the glad an-gels on Eden's fair plains; I want to be gathered with all the redeemed; Yes: o-ver the River where the fields are all green.

3 'Tis a land of rare beauty — a realm of delight,
O'erflowing with gladness, refulgent with light;
Its verdure ne'er withers, its flowers ne'er die,
O! I long to pass over with Jesus on high.

4 Its fountains are pure, and its pleasures untold,
Its fulness of rapture no tongue can unfold;
Its life-breathing zephyrs float gently along
O'er the River enticing a purified throng.

I LONG TO BE THERE.

G. D. BROWNE.

1. When I think of that city of light, And of crowns which the glorified wear;
2. It is not that I'm weary of pain, Or impatient, in tri-als and cares,
3. To that city my Saviour has gone, Rich mansions and crowns to prepare;

And of garments so pure and so white, Then I long, O I long to be there.
But I know that to die would be gain, And I long, O I long to be there.
For the hosts that are following on, And I long, O I long to be there.

CHORUS.

O, I long with the saints in light, To be clothed with the garments in white;
And in songs with the angels unite, Hallelujah, Hallelujah to the Lamb.

Conclusion of hymn on opposite page.

5 There the weary may rest, and the wicked ne'er come,
There the Saints are all safe in their heavenly home;
With their harps and their crowns they forever are seen,
Away o'er the River where the valleys are green.

6 'Tis Jesus invites me this glory to see,
To reign with him ever all happy and free;
I'll join with the ransomed, and with them abide,
I'll cross the dark River,—bright Angels will guide.

WILL YOU BE THERE? C. P. M.

J. W. D.

1. Beyond this life of hopes and fears, Beyond this world of griefs and tears,
There is a re-gion fair; It knows no change and no decay,
No night, but one un-end-ing day. Oh say, will you be there?

2. Its glorious gates are closed to sin: Nought that defiles can enter in
To mar its beau-ty rare; Up-on that bright, e-ternal shore,
Earth's bit-ter curse is known no more. Oh say, will you be there?

CHORUS. Ad lib.
Yes, we'll be there! yes, we'll be there! In that beauti-ful world of light!

3 No drooping form, no tearful eye,
No hoary head, no weary sigh,
   No pain, no grief, no care;
But joys which mortals may not know,
Like a calm river, ever flow.
   Oh say, will you be there?

4 Our Saviour, once as mortal child,
As mortal man, by man reviled,
   There many crowns doth wear;
While thousands thousands swell the strain
Of glory to the Lamb once slain!
   Oh say, will you be there?

5 Who shall be there? The lowly here:
All those who serve the Lord in fear,
   The world's proud mockery dare;
Who, by the Holy Spirit led,
Rejoice the narrow path to tread:—
   These, these shall all be there!

6 Will you be there? You shall, you must,
If, hating sin, in Christ you trust,
   Who did that place prepare.
Still doth his voice sound sweetly, "Come!
I am the way — I'll lead you home —
   With me, you shall be there!"

I WILL NOT LET THEE GO. 6 lines. 8s.

Music by REV. L. HARTSOUGH.

1. Come O thou Traveller unknown, Whom still I hold, but cannot see;
2. I need not tell thee who I am; My sin and mis-e-ry declare;

My com-pa-ny before is gone, And I am left alone with Thee:
Thyself hast called me by my name; Look on thy hands and read it there;

With thee all night I mean to stay, And wrestle till the break of day.
But who, I ask thee, who art thou? Tell me thy name, and tell me now.

3 In vain thou strugglest to get free:
   I never will unloose my hold:
   Art thou the Man that died for me?
   The secret of thy love unfold:
   Wrestling, I will not let thee go,
   Till I thy name, thy nature know.

4 Wilt thou not yet to me reveal
   Thy new, unutterable name?
   Tell me, I beseech thee, tell;—

To know it now resolved I am.
Wrestling, I will not let thee go,
Till I thy name, thy nature know.

5 What, tho' my shrinking flesh complain,
   And murmur to contend so long?
   I rise superior to my pain,
   When I am weak, then I am strong;
   And when my all of strength shall fail,
   I shall with the God-Man prevail.

LIFT ME HIGHER. 8s & 7s.

Music by Rev. L. Hartsough.

1. "Lift me higher! lift me higher!" From these scenes of pain and night!
Bear me up on angels' pinions, To the world of spirits bright.
Let not earth's de-lusive pleasures Serve my highest joys to blight;
I would range the fields of glo-ry In ce-les-tial worlds of light.

2. "Lift me higher! lift me higher!" When temptations me as-sail;
Arm me for the fiercest conflict, Let me in thy strength prevail.
"Lift me higher!" keep before me Calvary's Mount where Jesus died:
Rest my faith in Christ, my Saviour, My Redeem-er cru-ci-fied.

NEARER, MY GOD, TO THEE.

DR. L. MASON.
From "Sabbath Hymn and Tune Book," by permission.

2 Though like a wanderer,
  Daylight all gone,
  Darkness be over me,
  My rest a stone;
  Yet in my dreams I'd be,
  :|| Nearer, my God, to thee, ||:
  Nearer to thee.

3 There let the way appear
  Steps up to heaven;
  All that thou sendest me
  In mercy given,
  Angels to beckon me,
  :|| Nearer, my God, to thee, ||:
  Nearer to thee.

4 Then with my waking thoughts,
  Bright with thy praise,
  Out of my stony griefs,
  Bethel I'll raise;
  So by my woes to be
  :|| Nearer, my God, to thee, |:
  Nearer to thee.

5 Or if on joyful wing,
  Cleaving the sky,
  Sun, moon, and stars forgot,
  Upward I fly,
  Still all my song shall be
  :|| Nearer, my God, to thee, ||:
  Nearer to thee.

Conclusion of hymn on opposite page.

3 "Lift me higher! lift me higher!"
  In affliction's darkest hour
  Let my faith surmount the trial
  In the strength of Jesus' power.
  "Lift me higher! lift me higher!"
  Till by faith the land I see
  Where the ransomed from affliction,
  Grief, and pain are ever free.

4 When death's shadows gather round me,
  Plume my spirit for its flight
  To the land that knows no sorrow,
  Neither pain, nor death, nor night.
  "Lift me higher!" HIGHER! HIGHER!
  Till my spirit ends its flight
  Far beyond this world of darkness
  In the realms of endless light.
                          S. V. R. FORD.

THEY ARE WAITING FOR ME.

Words by Mrs. C. B. COWEL. J. W. D.

3 For I'm coming, darling, coming
　Feebly to the river-side,
　Where beside the same pale boatman,
　I shall cross the mystic tide.

4 When thro' weary hours I've counted
　Step by step time's solemn tramp,
　As the night hung dark and heavy,
　All the air pressed chill and damp.

5 Suddenly from o'er the river,
　Silvery chimes broke on my ear;
　Infant voices seemed to whisper,
　Hasten to us, mother dear!

6 Yes, my darlings; only waiting
　'Till our Father bids me come,
　Sitting by the bright glad river,
　Waiting to be carried home.

WHY NOT GO? 8s & 6s. 47

Words and Music by REV. L. HARTSOUGH.

1. Our Canaan fair with streets of gold, And wealth of pleasures all untold, You each with us may share; Its hopes are bright and never end, And an-gel bands will us at-tend; We hope to meet you there.
2. Its pearly gates that close us in, Shut out all sorrow, death and sin, And pain and anxious care; No burdened ones will walk those streets, Or sighing ones each oth-er greet; Why not go with us there?

3 The blessed Spirit bids you come;
O hasten now for yet there's room,
  And you a crown shall wear;
Neglecting Christ of Heaven you fail,
Obeying him you will prevail,
  And soon be with us there.

4 The royal road leads surely on
Thro' fightings oft, but victory's won,
  Yes, safe 'mid every snare;
The thronging angels fill the sky,
To cheer us on where none can die,—
  Why not go with us there?

THE PILGRIM'S LOT.

1 How happy is the pilgrim's lot;
How free from every anxious thought,
  From worldly hope and fear!
Confined to neither court nor cell,
His soul disdains on earth to dwell,
  He only sojourns here.

2 No foot of land do I possess,
No cottage in the wilderness;
  A poor wayfaring man,
I lodge awhile in tents below,
Or gladly wander to and fro,
  Till I my Canaan gain.

3 Nothing on earth I call my own;
A stranger to the world unknown,
  I all their goods despise:
I trample on their whole delight,
And seek a city out of sight,
  A city in the skies.

4 There is my house and portion fair,
My treasure and my heart are there,
  And my abiding home;
For me my elder brethren stay,
And angels beckon me away,
  And Jesus bids me come!

48. OUR LOVED ONES IN HEAVEN.

Words by REV. J. W. DADMUN. Music by LESSUR.

1. Come all ye saints to Pisgah's mountain, Come view your home beyond the tide;

Hear now the voices of your lov'd ones, What they sing on the other side,—

Second time CHORUS.

Some of bright crowns of glory are singing, Some of dear ones who stand near the shore

CHORUS. O the prospect! it is so transporting, And no danger I fear from the tide;

D.S.

For the fond heart must ever be clinging To the faithful we love ev-er-more.

Let me go to the home of the Christian, Let me stand robed in white by his side.

CHRIST OUR PILOT. 8s & 7s.

J. W. D.

1. Sailor, enter not life's voyage, Without compass, star or guide,
For its quicksands all around thee, Thick are strown on every side.
D.s. He's the star of consolation, And will guide him safely home.

CHORUS.
Jesus calm'd the raging ocean; And, where'er the sail or roams.

2 Smooth, serenely flow its waters,
But the sunken rocks are near,
Many a gallant bark hath foundered,
How wilt thou the danger clear.

3 See its circling eddies darken,
Wave on wave of passion rise,
Earth hath here no hand to guide thee,
Seek thy Pilot from the skies.

4 Seek, to thread thy path of danger,
Him who once in mortal form,
When the tempest raged in fury,
Trod the wave and stilled the storm.

5 He shall guide thee o'er the billow,
Thro' each changing wave of strife,
Till thy bark is safely anchored,
On the " crystal sea of life."

Miss S. A. Brown.

Conclusion of hymn on opposite page.

2 There endless springs of life are flowing,
There are the fields of living green;
Mansions of beauty are provided,
And the King of the saints is seen.
Soon my conflicts and toils will be ended;
I shall join those who've passed on before;
For my lov'd ones, O how I do miss them!
I must press on and meet them once more.

3 Faith now beholds the flowing river,
Coming from underneath the throne:
There, too, the Saviour reigns forever,
And he'll welcome the faithful home.
Would you sit by the banks of the river
With the friends you have lov'd by your side?
Would you join in the song of the angels?
Then be ready to follow your guide.

THE UNION BAND.

W. B. BRADBURY. By permission.

1. O we're a band of brethren dear, Who will join this happy band? Who live as pilgrim strangers here, Who will join this happy band?

CHORUS. Hal-le-lu-jah, hal-le-lu-jah, We will join this happy band, Singing Hal-le-lujah, hal-le-lu-ah, We will join this happy band.

2 The prophets and apostles too
  Once belonged to this happy band;
And all God's children here below,
  All have joined this happy band.
Cho.—Hallelujah, &c.

3 Let no contention e'er divide
  Members of this happy band;
But firm, united, side by side,
  Through this life together stand.
Cho.—Hallelujah, &c.

4 And when death comes, as come it must,
  To divide this happy band,
The links will not return to dust,
  They will shine at God's right hand.
Cho.—Hallelujah, &c.

THAT BEAUTIFUL RIVER. 51

J. W. D.

1. O have you not heard of a beautiful stream, That flows thro' our Father's land?
2. With murmuring sound doth it wander along, Thro' fields of e - ternal green;

Its waters gleam bright in the heavenly light, And ripple o'er golden sand.
Where songs of the blest, in their heaven of rest, Float soft on the air serene.

CHORUS.

Oh, seek that beau-ti - ful stream, Seek now that beau-ti - ful stream;

Its waters so free are flowing for thee; Oh, seek that beau-ti-ful stream.

3 Its fountains are deep, and its waters are pure,
    And sweet to the weary soul;
  It flows from the throne of Jehovah alone,
    Oh, come where its bright waves roll.

4 This beautiful stream is the River of Life!
    It flows for all nations, free!
  A balm for each wound in its water is found;
    Oh, sinner, it flows for thee!

5 Oh, will ye not drink of this beautiful stream,
    And dwell on its peaceful shore?
  The Spirit says "Come, all ye weary ones home,
    And wander in sin no more.

R. TORRY, JR.

GOING HOME.

WM. B. BRADBURY. By permission.

2 Why should we gather earth's withering flowers,
  When we're going, going, going home?
Soon shall we tread the fair Heavenly bowers,
  For we're going, going, going home;
There, fragrant garlands immortal will bloom,
Untouched by blight, and unshadowed by gloom,
And is ever strewing the path to the tomb;
  For we're going, going, going home.

3 Soon we shall hear the glad welcoming voice,
  We are going, going, going home;
Bidding our spirits ever rejoice,
  We are going, going, going home:
Home to our mansion prepared in the sky,
Where we can never more suffer or die.
O! let our anthem of praise ring on high!
  We are going, going, going home.

THE YEAR OF RELEASE.

J. W. D.

"The year of release is at hand."—DEUT. xv. 9.

2. Long, long, tho' fatigued and oppress'd
You have toil'd at your Master's command;
But soon you shall enter his rest,
For the year of release is at hand.

3 How fair are those mansions above!
The scenes that await you, how grand!
How thrilling the welcome of love!
And the year of release is at hand.

4 No storms of temptation or care
Sweep over that beautiful land;
But joys never-fading are there,
And the year of release is at hand.

5 Earth's pleasures are taking their flight,
But the glories celestial expand;
And faith almost changes to sight,
For the year of release is at hand!

GOD IS EVERY-WHERE. 7s.

J. W. D.

1. God is in the torrent's fall, In the summer breeze;
God is in the thunder's call, In the whisp'ring trees,
Where the low-ly violet springs, Where the faithful i-vy clings:
Where the small bird sweetly sings, There, forever, there is God.

2 God is in the flashing eye,
    In the speaking tongue;
  God is in the mourner's cry,
    In the marriage song—
  With the saint at morning praying,
  With the midnight murd'rer slaying,
  With the cradled infant playing,
  There, forever, there is God.

3 God is in the army's path,
    In the ocean's swell;
  God is in the whirlwind's wrath,
    In the tolling bell—
  By the sinner's dying bed,
  By the watcher's weary head,
  By the living and the dead,
  There, forever there is God.

JESUS PAID IT ALL.

1. Nought of mer-it, or of price, Remains to Jus-tice due;
2. When he from his lofty throne, Stooped down to do and die,

Je-sus died, and paid it all—Yes, all the debt I owe.
Ev'-ry thing was ful-ly done; "'Tis finished!" was his cry.

CHORUS.

Je-sus paid it all— Paid all the debt I owe,

Je-sus died and paid it all, Yes, all the debt I owe.

3 Weary, working, plodding one,
   O, wherefore toil you so?
  Cease your " doing;" all was done,
   Done ages long ago.
    Jesus paid it all, &c.

4 'Till, to Jesus' work you cling,
   Alone by simple faith,
  " Doing" is a deadly thing,

Your " doing" ends in death.
    Jesus paid it all, &c.

5 Cast your deadly " doing" down,
   Down, all at Jesus' feet;
  Stand in him, in him alone,
   All glorious and complete.
    Jesus paid it all, &c.

THE CHRISTIAN HERO.

REV. E. H. NEVIN.

1. Live on the field of battle! Be earnest in the fight;
   Stand forth with manly courage, And struggle for the right.
2. Watch on the field of battle! The foe is ev'rywhere;
   His fiery darts fly thickly, Like lightning thro' the air.

CHORUS.
Live! live! live! Live on the field of battle!
Watch! watch! watch! Watch on the field of battle!

THE CHRISTIAN HERO.

3 Pray on the field of battle!
   God works with those who pray;
   His mighty arm can nerve us,
   And make us win the day.
   Pray! pray! pray!
   Pray on the field of battle!

4 Die on the field of battle!
   'Tis noble thus to die;
   God smiles on valiant soldiers,
   Their record is on high.
   Die! die! die!
   Die on the field of battle!

THEN ROLL, ROLL AWAY. 57

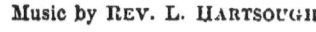

With spirit.

1. I'm looking for Je-sus, My Saviour and King, To change this vile body, and cause me to sing Where life's crystal river e-ter-nally glides,

CHORUS.

And ev-er-green verdure grows up by its side. Then roll, roll away! Old Time hasten thro', And bear me, dear Saviour, to joys ev-er new.

2 I'm hoping in Jesus that soon I shall see
A world bathed in glory, a soil that is free,
Where the toil-worn and weary forever will sing
Loud anthems of praises to Jesus, our King.

3 I'm waiting for Jesus, who soon will appear,
To waken my kindred that I love so dear;
And give us a home with the pure and the bless'd,
In the realms of fair Canaan forever to rest.

4 I'm longing for Jesus to end this rude strife,
Which shades us with sorrow embittering life;
I weep over follies the pathway I tread,
O'er hopes often blasted, and friends that are dead.

5 I'm sighing for Jesus, old earth has grown drear,
And wait for the hour when he shall appear,
To make it his home ever beauteous and fair,
I long to behold it, I sigh to be there.

PORT OF GLORY.

J. W. D.

1. Lo, the Gospel ship is sail-ing, Bound for Canaan's happy shore;
All who wish to sail for glo-ry, Come and welcome, rich and poor.

CHORUS.
Glo-ry! glory! Hal-le-lu-jah: All the sailors loudly cry,
See the blissful ports of Glo-ry, Opening to each blissful eye.

2 Thousands she has safely landed,
  Far beyond this mortal shore,
Thousands yet are sailing in her,
  Yet there's room for thousands more.

3 Richly laden with provisions,
  Want her sailors never know;
Gospel grace, and every blessing,
  From her noble Pilot flow.

4 Sails well filled with heavenly breezes,
  Swiftly waft the ship along;
All her company rejoicing—
  Glory! bursts from every tongue.

ONWARD AND UPWARD.

REV. G. ROBBINS.

3 Bear the cross, Christian,
  Follow thy Master;
Bright the crown, Christian
  Haste thee on faster.
Onward and upward,
  Still be thine endeavor;
The rest that remaineth,
  Shall be forever.

4 Lift the eye, Christian,
  Just as it closeth;
Raise the heart, Christian,
  Ere it reposeth;
Onward and upward,
  Still be thine endeavor;
The rest that remaineth,
  Shall be forever.

WAITING FOR THE BOATMAN. 8s & 7s.

J. W. D.

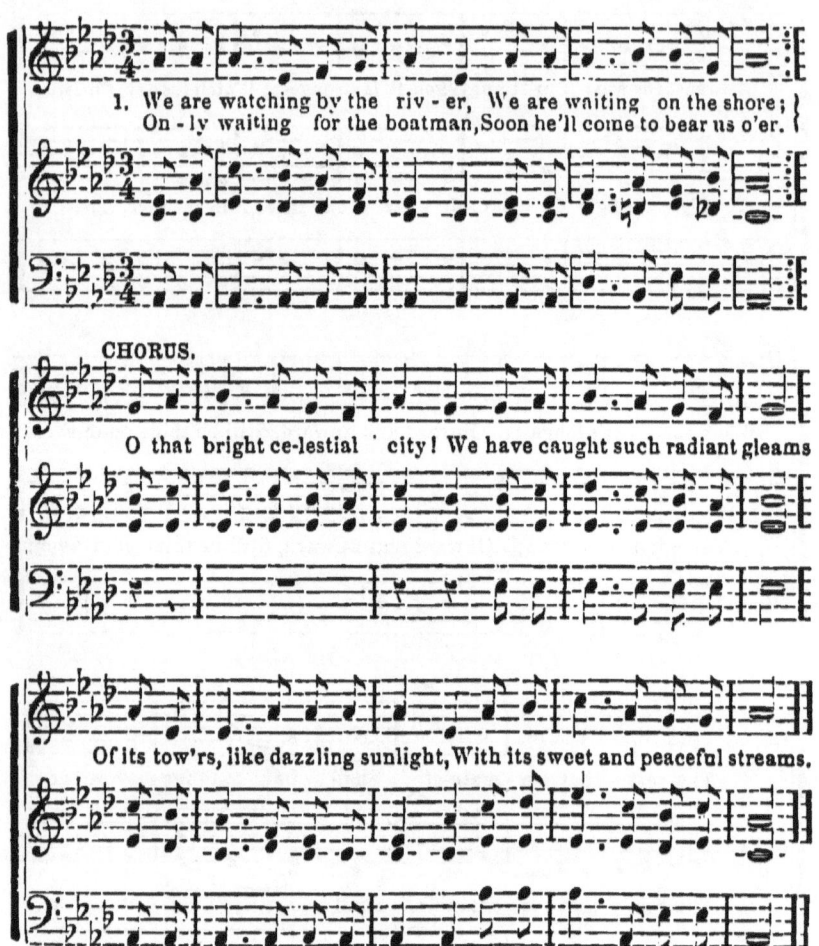

1. We are watching by the riv-er, We are waiting on the shore;
On-ly waiting for the boatman, Soon he'll come to bear us o'er.

CHORUS.

O that bright ce-lestial city! We have caught such radiant gleams
Of its tow'rs, like dazzling sunlight, With its sweet and peaceful streams.

2 He has called for many a loved one,
　We have seen them leave our side;
With our Saviour we shall meet them,
　When we too have crossed the tide.

3 Though the mist hangs o'er the river,
　And its billows loudly roar,
Yet we hear the song of angels,
　Wafted from the other shore,

4 When we've passed that vale of shadows
　With its dark and chilling tide,
In that bright and glorious city
　We shall evermore abide.

5 So we're marching by the river,
　We are watching on the shore,
Only waiting for the boatman,
　Soon he'll come to bear us o'er.

OUR SOLDIER BOY IS MISSING.* 61

Words and Music by REV. L. HARTSOUGH

2 Where we go, how much remind us
   Of the dear one whom we love;
But they tell us nobly, bravely,
   He at duty's call did move.
In the camp was loving, prayerful,
   On the battle-field was brave;
And with pride we hear them tell us,
   Honored is our soldier's grave.

3 Ah! he lies before Port Hudson,
   With the brave who nobly fell,
As the iron hail was strewing
   With the dead both hill and dell.
Cherished is the mem'ry left us,
   Round our hearts still clings his love;
And we hope soon to embrace him,
   In the realms of light above.

* In memory of JOHN D. WEST, who fell, June 14, 1863, 'mid the fiercest of that last and fearful charge made upon Port Hudson before its fall.

DID CHRIST O'ER SINNERS WEEP?

J. W. D.

1. Did Christ o'er sinners weep, And shall our cheeks be dry?
2. The Son of God in tears, The wond'ring an-gels see;

Let floods of pen-i-ten-tial grief Burst forth from every eye.
Be thou as-tonish'd, O my soul; He shed those tears for thee.
D.S. In heav'n a-lone no sin is found, And there's no weeping there.

CHORUS.
He wept that we might weep; Each sin demands a tear;

The heart of stone.

1. O that I could repent,
   With all my idols part,
   And to thy gracious eye present
   An humble, contrite heart.

2. A heart with grief opprest,
   For having grieved my God;
   A troubled heart, that cannot rest
   Till sprinkled with thy blood.

3. Jesus, on me bestow
   The penitent desire;
   With true sincerity of wo,
   My aching breast inspire.

4. With soft'ning pity look,
   And melt my hardness down:
   Strike with thy love's resistless stroke,
   And break this heart of stone.

SWEET HOUR OF PRAYER. L, M. Double. 63

From "The Golden Chain." By permission. W. B. BRADBURY.

2 Sweet hour of prayer! sweet hour of prayer!
Thy wings shall my petition bear
To him whose truth and faithfulness,
Engage the waiting soul to bless;
And since he bids me seek his face,
Believe his word, and trust his grace,
I'll cast on him my every care,
And wait for thee, sweet hour of pray'r!

3 Sweet hour of prayer! sweet hour of prayer!
May I thy consolation share,
Till, from Mount Pisgah's lofty height,
I view my home, and take my flight!
This robe of flesh I'll drop, and rise
To seize the everlasting prize;
And shout, while passing thro' the air,
Farewell, farewell, sweet hour of pray'r!

JOURNEYING HOME TO HEAVEN

Words and Music by Jas. M. Stewart.

1. We're journeying home to heaven, Will you go? will you go?
Where sins are all for-giv-en, Will you go? will you go?
There Je-sus waits to welcome us, And crowns of life be-stow,
And a home among the angels; Will you go? will you go?

2 The loved and blest are waiting,
   Will you go? will you go?
Our sorrows contemplating,
   Will you go? will you go?
They tell us all is peaceful there,
   And tears no longer flow,
And the songs are never ending;
   Will you go? will you go?

3 O, soon will be that meeting,
   Will you go? will you go?
And blest will be that greeting,
   Will you go? will you go?
There parting never more is known,
   Like farewells here below,
Where our God again unites us;
   Will you go? will you go?

4 Then let us join in singing,
   Will you go? will you go?
While homeward we are winging;
   Will you go? will you go?
The dove of old returned no more,
   When ceased the water's flow,
From her home beyond the mountains,
   Will you go? will you go?

WHAT SHALL I DO TO BE SAVED?

J. W. D.

1. O! what shall I do to be saved From the sor-rows that bur-den my soul? Like the waves in the storm When the winds are at war, Chilling floods of distress o'er me roll.

2. O! what shall I do to be saved, When the pleasures of youth are all fled? And the friends I have loved, From the earth are removed, And I weep o'er the graves of the dead.

3 O! what shall I do to be saved,
When sickness my strength shall subdue?
Or the world in a day,
Like a cloud roll away,
And eternity opens to view.

4 O! Lord look in mercy on me,
Come, O come and speak peace to my soul;
Unto whom shall I flee,
Dearest Lord, but to thee,
Thou canst make my poor broken heart whole.

SHALL WE MEET? 8s & 7s.

By permission of G. D. RUSSELL & CO.

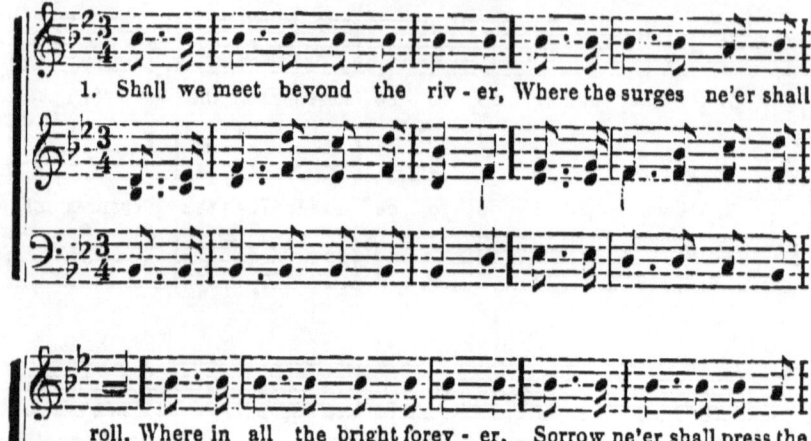

1. Shall we meet beyond the riv-er, Where the surges ne'er shall roll, Where in all the bright forev-er, Sorrow ne'er shall press the

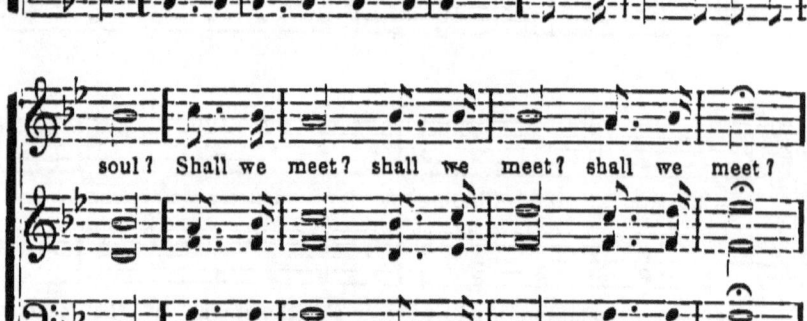

soul? Shall we meet? shall we meet? shall we meet?

2 Shall we meet in that blest harbor,
   When our stormy voyage is o'er?
Shall we meet and cast our anchor,
   By the fair celestial shore?
      Shall we meet? &c.

3 Shall we meet in yonder city,
   Where the towers of crystal shine,
Where the walls are all of jasper,
   Built by workmanship divine?
      Shall we meet? &c.

4 Shall we meet with many a lov'd one,
   That was torn from our embrace?
Shall we listen to their voices,
   And behold them face to face?
      Shall we meet? &c.

SHALL WE MEET? Concluded. 67

CHORUS, AND ANSWER.

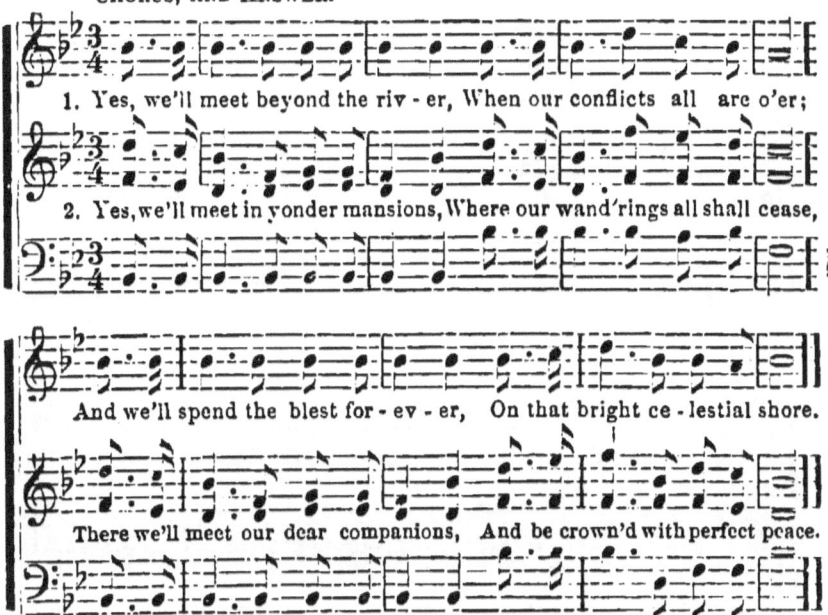

1. Yes, we'll meet beyond the riv-er, When our conflicts all are o'er;
2. Yes, we'll meet in yonder mansions, Where our wand'rings all shall cease,

And we'll spend the blest for-ev-er, On that bright ce-lestial shore.
There we'll meet our dear companions, And be crown'd with perfect peace.

3 Yes, we'll meet, where bliss immortal
  Sweeter far than rest can be;
  And before the throne eternal,
  All our earthly triumphs see.

4 Yes, we'll meet, where all is onward,
  Every change new glories bring;
  And the host still moving forward,
  Glorify our heavenly King.

OLD HUNDRED. L. M.

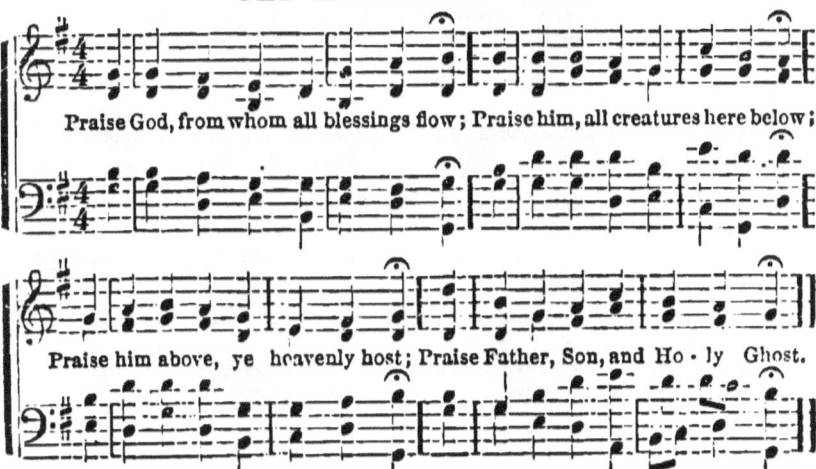

Praise God, from whom all blessings flow; Praise him, all creatures here below;
Praise him above, ye heavenly host; Praise Father, Son, and Ho-ly Ghost.

SILOAM. C. M.

I. B. WOODBURY. By permission.

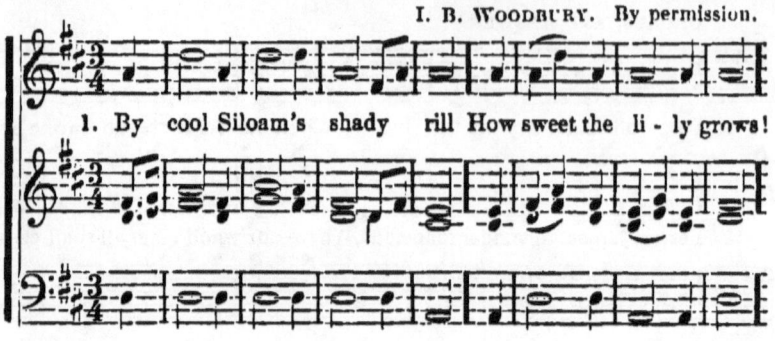

1. By cool Siloam's shady rill How sweet the li-ly grows!

How sweet the breath, beneath the hill, Of Sharon's dewy rose!

The Christian Child.

2 Lo! such the child whose early feet
  The paths of peace have trod;
Whose secret heart, with influence sweet,
  Is upward drawn to God.

3 By cool Siloam's shady rill
  The lily must decay;
The rose that blooms beneath the hill
  Must shortly fade away.

4 And soon, too soon the wintry hour
  Of man's maturer age
Will shake the soul with sorrow's power,
  And stormy passion's rage.

5 O Thou who givest life and breath,
  We seek thy grace alone,
In childhood, manhood, age, and death,
  To keep us still thine own.

Death gain to the faithful.

1 Why should our tears in sorrow flow
  When God recalls his own,
And bids them leave a world of wo,
  For an immortal crown?

2 Is not e'en death a gain to those
  Whose life to God was given?
Gladly to earth their eyes they close,
  To open them in heaven.

3 Their toils are past, their work is done,
  And they are fully blest;
They fought the fight, the victory won,
  And entered into rest.

4 Then let our sorrows cease to flow;
  God has recalled his own;
But let our hearts, in every wo,
  Still say,—Thy will be done.

HEBER. C. M. 69

Geo. Kingsley. By permission.

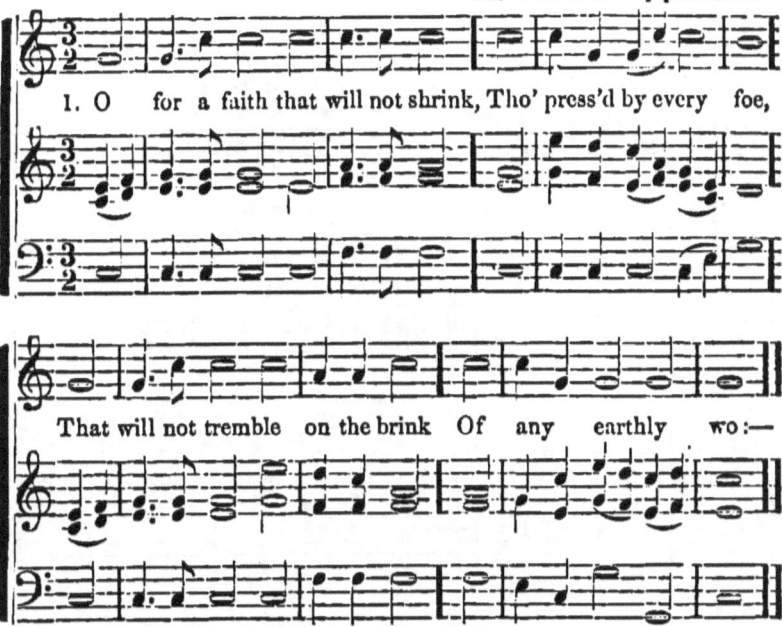

1. O for a faith that will not shrink, Tho' press'd by every foe, That will not tremble on the brink Of any earthly wo:—

For victorious faith.

2 That will not murmur or complain
   Beneath the chast'ning rod,
   But, in the hour of grief or pain,
   Will lean upon its God;—

3 A faith that shines more bright and clear
   When tempests rage without;
   That when in danger knows no fear,
   In darkness feels no doubt;—

4 That bears, unmoved, the world's dread frown,
   Nor heeds its scornful smile;
   That seas of trouble cannot drown,
   Or Satan's arts beguile;—

5 A faith that keeps the narrow way
   Till life's last hour is fled,
   And with a pure and heavenly ray
   Illumes a dying bed.

6 Lord, give us such a faith as this,
   And then, whate'er may come,
   We'll taste, e'en here, the hallow'd bliss
   Of an eternal home.

The only solace in sorrow.

1 O Thou who driest the mourner's tear,
   How dark this world would be,
   If, when deceived and wounded here,
   We could not fly to thee.

2 The friends who in our sunshine live,
   When winter comes, are flown;
   And he who has but tears to give,
   Must weep those tears alone.

3 But Christ can heal that broken heart,
   Which, like the plants that throw
   Their fragrance from the wounded part,
   Breathes sweetness out of wo.

4 O, who could bear life's stormy doom,
   Did not His wing of love
   Come brightly wafting thro' the gloom
   Our peace-branch from above.

5 Then sorrow, touch'd by Him, grows bright
   With more than rapture's ray;
   As darkness shows us worlds of light,
   We never saw by day.

HADDAM. H. M.

ENGLISH. Ar. by DR. MASON.

1. The Lord Jehovah reigns, His throne is built on high;
The garments he assumes............ Are light and majesty:
His glories shine with beams so bright, No mortal eye can bear the sight.

Greatness and condescension.

2 The thunders of his hand
  Keep the wide world in awe;
  His wrath and justice stand
    To guard his holy law;
And where his love resolves to bless,
His truth confirms and seals the grace.

3 Through all his mighty works
  Amazing wisdom shines:
  Confounds the powers of hell,
    And all their dark designs;
Strong is his arm, and shall fulfil
His great decrees and sovereign will.

4 And will this sovereign King
  Of glory condescend;—
  And will he write his name,
    My Father and my Friend?
I love his Name, I love his word;
Join all my powers to praise the Lord.

Conclusion of hymn on opposite page.

2 No weary days I then shall know,
  No night of grief and care,
  The shining robes of righteousness,
    Each happy saint shall wear,
And I shall see my Master's face,
  The Lord I love below,
Thorn-crowned and crucified for me,—
  Oh how I long to go!

3 There shall I from my labors rest,
  No fears nor doubts I'll know;
But gladly through the golden streets,
  With song and shout I'll go.

When will the Angel come for me,
  When shall I upward soar,
When shall I scale the heavenly heights,
  And tread the earth no more?

4 No tear shall dim the eyes that gaze
  Upon the glories there,
Each saint who suffered with the Lord,
  His joyful reign shall share.
No sin shall mar the sacred joy,
  No parting tear shall flow,
There all God's ransomed children meet,
  Oh how I long to go!

JOYFULLY.

Rev. A. D. Merrill.

1. Joyfully, joyfully, onward I move, Bound for the land of bright spirits a-bove;
Angelic choristers sing as I come, Joyful-ly, joyful-ly haste to thy home.
Soon with my pilgrimage ended below, Home to that land of delight will I go,
Pilgrim and stranger, no more shall I roam, Joyful-ly, joyfully resting at home.

2.
Friends fondly cherished have passed on before;
Waiting, they watch me approaching that shore;
Singing, to cheer me through death's chilling gloom,
Joyfully, joyfully haste to thy home:
Sounds of sweet melody fall on my ear;
Harps of the blessed, your voices I hear!
Rings with the harmony heaven's high dome,
Joyfully, joyfully haste to thy home.

CONWAY. C. M.

1. Come, let us join our cheerful songs With angels round the throne; Ten thousand thousand are their tongues, Ten thousand thousand are their tongues, But all their joys are one.

2. Worthy the Lamb that died, they cry, To be exalted thus: Worthy the Lamb, our hearts reply, Worthy the Lamb, our hearts reply, For he was slain for us.

3 Jesus is worthy to receive
Honor and power divine;
And blessings more than we can give,
Be, Lord, forever thine.

4 The whole creation join in one,
To bless the sacred Name
Of Him that sits upon the throne,
And to adore the Lamb.

Conclusion of hymn on opposite page.

3 Death, with thy weapons of war, lay me low:
Strike, king of terrors, I fear not the blow;
Jesus hath broken the bars of the tomb;
Joyfully, joyfully, will I go home;
Bright will the morn of eternity dawn;
Death shall be banished, his sceptre be gone;
Joyfully then shall I witness his doom;
Joyfully, joyfully, safely at home.

WARE. L. M.

GEO. KINGSLEY By permission.

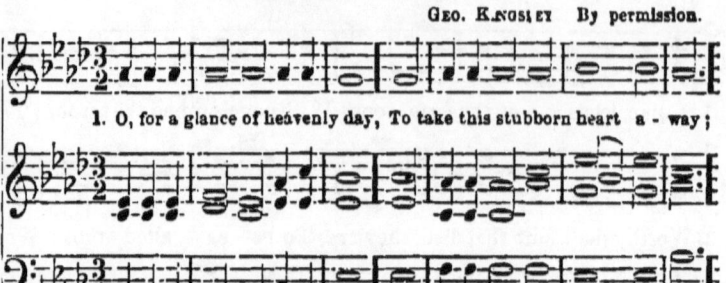

1. O, for a glance of heavenly day, To take this stubborn heart a-way;

And thaw, with beams of love divine, This heart, this frozen heart of mine.

The stubborn heart.

2 The rocks can rend; the earth can quake;
The seas can roar; the mountains shake;
Of feeling, all things show some sign,
But this unfeeling heart of mine.

3 To hear the sorrows thou hast felt,
O Lord, an adamant would melt;
But I can read each moving line,
And nothing moves this heart of mine.

4 Thy judgments, too, which devils fear—
Amazing thought! unmoved I hear;
Goodness and wrath in vain combine
To stir this stupid heart of mine.

5 But power divine can do the deed;
And, Lord, that power I greatly need:
Thy Spirit can from dross refine,
And melt and change this heart of mine.

The only plea.

1 Jesus, the sinner's friend, to thee,
Lost and undone, for aid I flee;
Weary of earth, myself, and sin;
Open thine arms, and take me in.

2 Pity and heal my sin-sick soul;
'Tis thou alone canst make me whole;
Dark, till in me thine image shine,
And lost, I am, till thou art mine.

3 At last I own it cannot be
That I should fit myself for thee:
Here, then, to thee I all resign;
Thine is the work, and only thine.

4 What shall I say thy grace to move!
Lord, I am sin,—but thou art love:
I give up every plea beside,—
Lord, I am lost—but thou hast died

CENTENARY HYMN. L. M.   75

Poetry by REV. GEO. LANSING TAYLOR.*   Arr. by REV. C. W. BALLOU.

Centenary Hymn.

1 Great God of Israel, Lo, to thee
Adoring millions bow the knee,
And bless, with rapturous shouts and tears
Thy goodness through a hundred years!

2 Since first our sires this New World trod,
What wonders hast thou wrought, O God!
A nation, vast from sea to sea:
A church, whose myriads worship thee.

3 God of Elijah, flash thy fire
Responsive, while our prayers aspire,
Till hearts and holocausts shall flame
A sacrifice to Jesus' name.

4 Pour forth thy spirit from on high!
Convert, illumine, sanctify!
Till millions more, with Israel's host,
Praise Father, Son, and Holy Ghost!

My heart is fixed.

1 My heart is fixed on thee, my God;
I rest my hope on thee alone;
I'll spread thy sacred truths abroad,—
To all mankind thy love make known.

2 Awake, my tongue; awake, my lyre;
With morning's earliest dawn arise;
To songs of joy my soul inspire,
And swell your music to the skies.

3 With those who in thy grace abound,
To thee I'll raise my thankful voice;
Till every land, the earth around,
Shall hear, and in thy Name rejoice.

4 Eternal God, celestial King,
Exalted be thy glorious Name:
Let hosts in heaven thy praises sing,
And saints on earth thy love proclaim.

* Composed for the Methodist Centennial Jubilee, held in Boston Music Hall, June 7th, 1866.

IS IT TRUE? 7s. 77

J. W. D.

1. Is it true that I must lie In the grave-yard bye-and-bye,
And with others, gone before, Sleep till time shall be no more?
Is it true? Oh, is it true?

2. Is it true, as many say, Life is but a passing day,
And that heaven is lost or won, Ere this fleeting day has flown?
Is it true? Oh, is it true?

3 Is it true that on the cross,
Jesus bled and died for us,
And, while hanging on the tree,
Upward sent a prayer for me?
Is it true? Oh, is it true?

4 Is it true that all death's slain
Will arise and live again,
And to final judgment go,
Some for bliss and some for woe?
Is it true? Oh, is it true?

HODGES REED.

Conclusion of hymn on opposite page.

2 O how blessed is this station!
Low before the cross I'll lie,
While I see divine compassion
Pleading in the victim's eye;
Here I'll sit, forever viewing,
Mercy streaming in his blood:
Precious drops, my soul bedewing,
Plead and claim my peace with God.

3 Here it is I find my heaven,
While upon the Lamb I gaze;'
Here I see my sins forgiven,
Lost in wonder, love, and praise.
May I still enjoy this feeling,
In all need to Jesus go;
Prove each day his blood more healing,
And Himself more deeply know.

78. A CLOSER WALK WITH GOD. C. M.

WIESENTHAL.

1. O for a closer walk with God, A calm and heavenly frame;
A light to shine up-on the road That leads me to the Lamb.
Where is the blessed-ness I knew, When first I saw the Lord?
Where is the soul-re-fresh-ing view Of Je-sus and his word?

MARTYN. 7s.

S. D. MARSH.

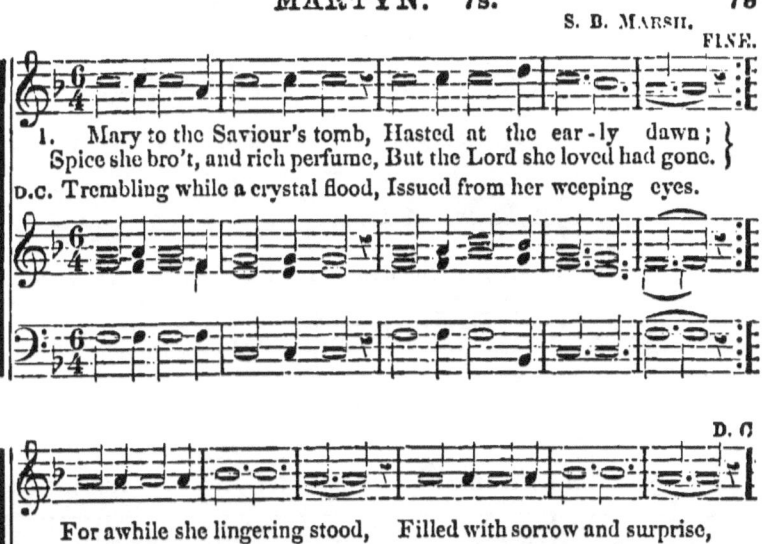

1. Mary to the Saviour's tomb, Hasted at the ear-ly dawn;
Spice she bro't, and rich perfume, But the Lord she loved had gone.
D.C. Trembling while a crystal flood, Issued from her weeping eyes.

For awhile she lingering stood, Filled with sorrow and surprise,

2 But her sorrows quickly fled,
  When she heard his welcome voice;
Christ had risen from the dead—
  Now he bids her heart rejoice.
What a change his word can make,
  Turning darkness into day;
Ye who weep for Jesus' sake,
  He will wipe your tears away.

3 He who came to comfort her,
  When she thought her all was lost,
Will for your relief appear,
  Though you now are tempest-tossed.
On his arm your burden cast;
  On his love your thoughts employ;
Weeping for a while may last,
  But the morning brings the joy.

Conclusion of hymn on opposite page.

2 What peaceful hours I once enjoyed,
  How sweet their memory still!
But they have left an aching void,
  The world can never fill.
Return, O holy Dove, return!
  Sweet messenger of rest!
I hate the sins that made thee mourn,
  And drove thee from my breast.

3 The dearest idol I have known,
  Whate'er that idol be,
Help me to tear it from thy throne,
  And worship only thee.
So shall my walk be close with God,
  Calm and serene my frame;
So purer light shall mark the road
  That leads me to the Lamb.

80 THE SINNER'S INVITATION. 6s & 7s.

By permission, from "Wesleyan Sacred Harp."

1. Sinner go, will you go To the highlands of heaven?
And the leaves of the bowers In the breezes are flitting.
Where the storms never blow, And the long summer's given;
Where the bright blooming flowers Are their o-dors e-mitting.

2 Where the saints robed in white,
  Cleansed in life's flowing fountain,
Shining beauteous and bright,
  Shall inhabit the mountain.
Where no sin nor dismay,
  Neither trouble nor sorrow,
Shall be felt for a day,
  Nor be feared for the morrow.

3 He's prepared thee a home;
  Sinner, canst thou believe it?
And invites thee to come;
  Sinner, wilt thou receive it?
O come, sinner, come,
  For the tide is receding,
And the Saviour will soon
  And forever cease pleading.

PETERBORO'. C. M.

1. Once more, my soul, the rising day Salutes thy waking eyes;
Once more, my voice, thy tribute pay To Him that rules the skies.

Morning: Self-consecration.

1 Once more, my soul, the rising day
 Salutes thy waking eyes;
 Once more, my voice, thy tribute pay
 To Him that rules the skies.

2 Night unto night his name repeats,
 The day renews the sound;
 Wide as the heavens on which he sits,
 To turn the seasons round.

3 'Tis he supports my mortal frame;
 My tongue shall speak his praise;
 My sins might rouse his wrath to flame,
 But yet his wrath delays.

4 O God, let all my hours be thine,
 Whilst I enjoy the light;
 Then shall my sun in smiles decline,
 And bring a peaceful night.

Instructing the young.

1 Delightful work! young souls to win,
 And turn the rising race
 From the deceitful paths of sin,
 To seek redeeming grace.

2 Children our kind protection claim;
 And God will well approve
 When infants learn to lisp his name,
 And their Redeemer love.

3 Be ours the bliss, in wisdom's way
 To guide untutored youth,
 And show the mind which went astray
 The Way, the Life, the Truth.

4 Almighty God, thine influence shed,
 To aid this blest design;
 The honors of thy name be spread,
 And all the glory thine

"FOREVER WITH THE LORD." S. M.

I. B. Woodbury. By permission

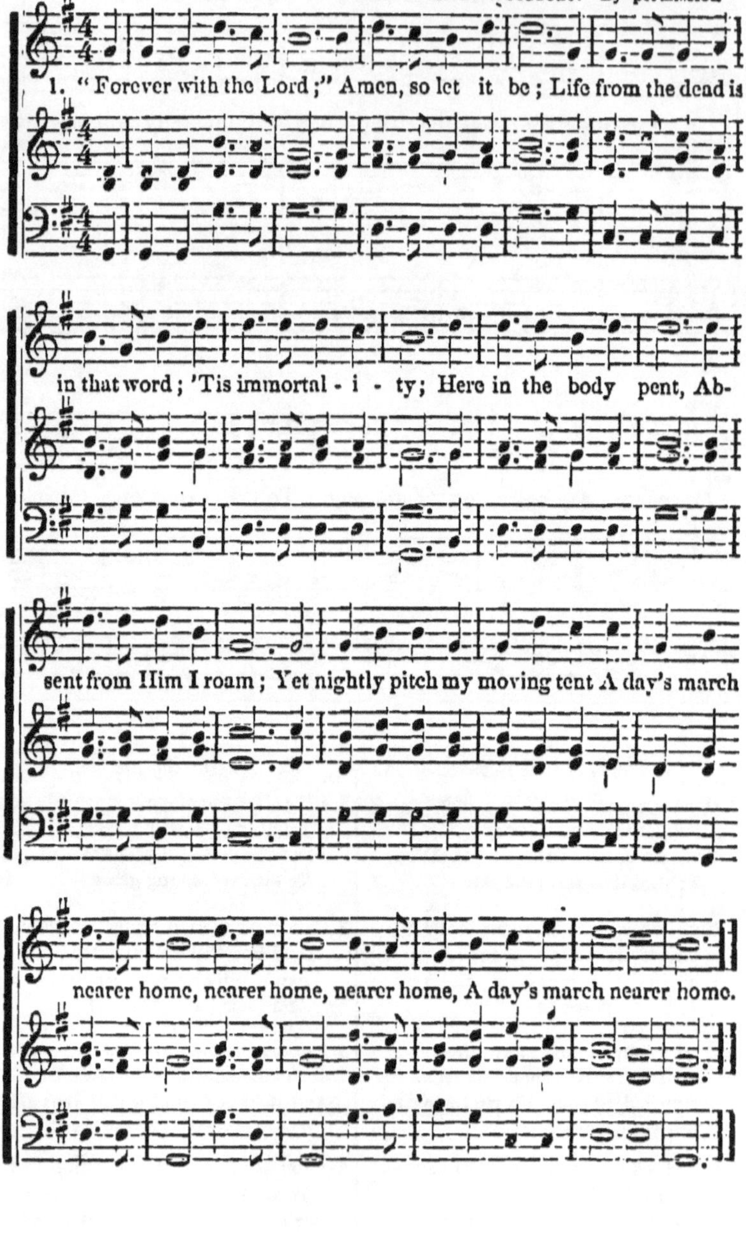

1. "Forever with the Lord;" Amen, so let it be; Life from the dead is in that word; 'Tis immortal-i-ty; Here in the body pent, Absent from Him I roam; Yet nightly pitch my moving tent A day's march nearer home, nearer home, nearer home, A day's march nearer home.

COME, YE DISCONSOLATE. 11s & 10s.

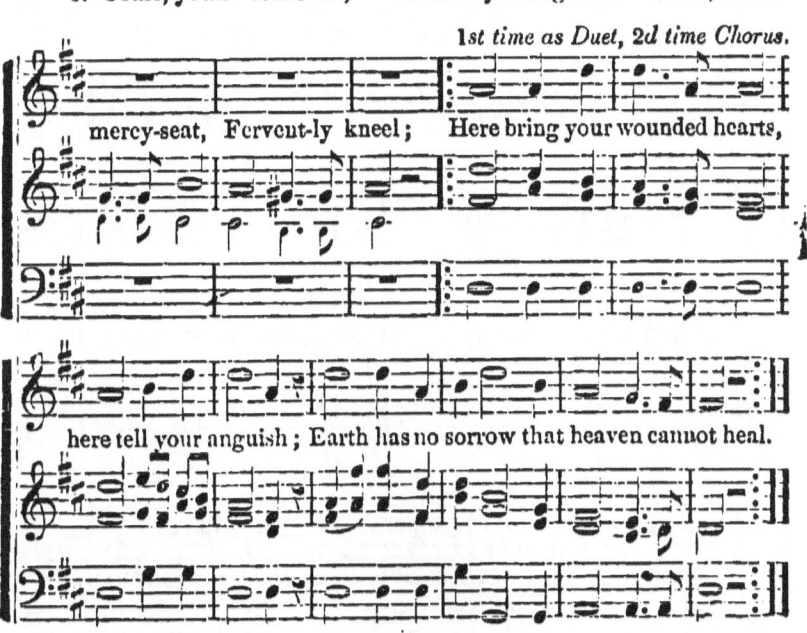

2 Joy of the desolate, light of the straying,
Hope of the penitent, fadeless and pure,—
Here speaks the Comforter, tenderly saying,—
Earth has no sorrow that Heaven cannot cure.

3 Here see the bread of life; see waters flowing
Forth from the throne of God, pure from above;
Come to the feast of love; come, ever knowing—
Earth has no sorrow but heaven can remove.

Conclusion of hymn on opposite page.

2 My Father's house on high,
  Home of my soul, how near,
At times, to faith's aspiring eye,
  Thy golden gates appear!
Ah, then my spirit faints,
  To reach the land I love;
The bright inheritance of saints,
  My heavenly home above.

3 Yet doubts still intervene,
  And all my comfort flies;
Like Noah's dove I flit between
  Rough seas and stormy skies;
Anon the clouds depart,
  The winds and waters cease,
While sweetly o'er my gladdened heart
  Expands the bow of peace.

WEBB. 7s & 6s.

G. J. Webb.

1. The morning light is breaking, The darkness disappears; The sons of earth are waking To penitential tears; Each breeze that sweeps the ocean Brings tidings from afar, Of nations in commotion, Prepared for Sion's war.

2 Rich dews of grace come o'er us,
   In many a gentle shower,
   And brighter scenes before us
   Are opening every hour:
   Each cry to heaven going,
   Abundant answer brings,
   And heavenly gales are blowing,
   With peace upon their wings.

3 See heathen nations bending
   Before the God we love,
   And thousand hearts ascending
   In gratitude above;
   While sinners, now confessing,
   The gospel's call obey,
   And seek the Saviour's blessing—
   A nation in a day.

4 Blest river of salvation,
   Pursue thy onward way:
   Flow thou to every nation,
   Nor in thy richness stay:
   Stay not till all the lowly
   Triumphant reach their home,
   Stay not till all the holy
   Proclaim the Lord is come.

LOOSE THE CABLE, LET ME GO.

2 Holy angels round me hover,
  Their light forms I almost see;
Golden harp and crown immortal,
  They are holding out to me;
Endless joys, eternal pleasures,
  Soon on me they will bestow;
From their presence do not keep me,
  Loose the cable, let me go.

3 But a little season only,
  Ere the hearts that here are one,
Shall forever be united
  In the realm beyond the sun.

Love cannot be quenched by dying,
  But will stronger, purer grow;
Wipe away the tears at parting,
  Loose the cable, let me go.

4 When so near the Holy City,
  Even at its pearly gate,
While its songs are wafted to me,
  Would you have me longer wait?
O, the joy that fills this moment,
  O, the happiness I know!
Seek no longer to detain me,
  Loose the cable, let me go.

HOME AT LAST.

J. W. D.

Words by Mrs. G. A. Hulse M'Leod.—Sung at the grave of Bishop Waugh.

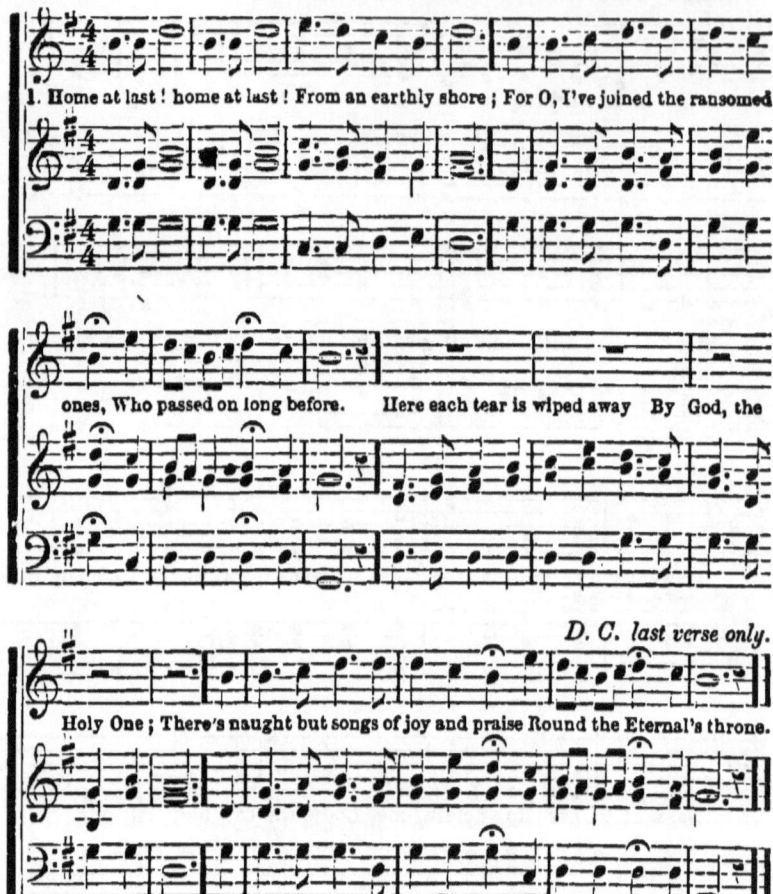

1. Home at last! home at last! From an earthly shore; For O, I've joined the ransomed ones, Who passed on long before. Here each tear is wiped away By God, the Holy One; There's naught but songs of joy and praise Round the Eternal's throne.

D. C. last verse only.

2 The pure in heart! the pure in heart!
  Robed in spotless white,
Are here with starry crowns of joy,
  All gloriously bright.
Some I loved so long ago,
  Who left me sad and lone,
I meet among the heavenly host,
  Within our Father's home.

3 Safe at home! safe at home!
  O, let the echo go,
To soothe the hearts that mourn me yet,
  In that first home below.
His dear arms are round me now,
  Who was for sinners slain;
Through him I've won eternal life;
  For me to die was gain.
Safe at home! safe at home!
  From an earthly shore;
I'll bless and praise thee, O my God,
  Forever, evermore.

THE BLEEDING SAVIOUR. C. M. 87

1. Behold the Saviour of mankind Nailed to the shameful tree;

Cho. The Lamb, the Lamb, the loving Lamb, The Lamb on Calva - ry!

How vast the love that him inclined To bleed and die for thee!

The Lamb was slain, but lives again, To in - ter - cede for me.

He died for thee.

2 Hark, how he groans, while nature shakes,
And earth's strong pillars bend:
The temple's vail in sunder breaks,—
The solid marbles rend.

3 'Tis done! the precious ransom's paid!
Receive my soul! he cries;
See where he bows his sacred head;
He bows his head and dies.

4 But soon he'll break death's envious chain,
And in full glory shine; [chain,
O Lamb of God, was ever pain,
Was ever love, like thine?

Godly sorrow at the cross.

1 Alas! and did my Saviour bleed?
And did my Sov'reign die?
Would he devote that sacred head
For such a worm as I?

2 Was it for crimes that I have done,
He groaned upon the tree?
Amazing pity! grace unknown!
And love beyond degree!

3 Well might the sun in darkness hide,
And shut his glories in,
When Christ, the mighty Maker, died,
For man, the creature's sin.

4 Thus might I hide my blushing face
While his dear cross appears;
Dissolve my heart in thankfulness,
And melt mine eyes to tears.

5 But drops of grief can ne'er repay
The debt of love I owe:
Here, Lord, I give myself away,—
'Tis all that I can do.

DEDHAM. C. M.

Gardner.

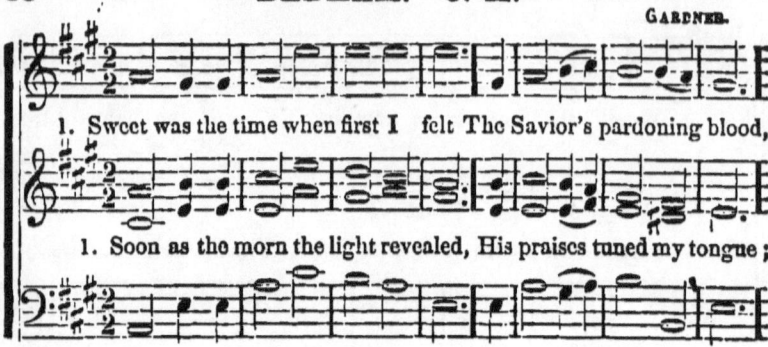

1. Sweet was the time when first I felt The Savior's pardoning blood,
Applied to cleanse my soul from guilt, And bring me home to God.

1. Soon as the morn the light revealed, His praises tuned my tongue;
And, when the evening shades prevailed, His love was all my song.

Mourning departed joys.

3 In prayer my soul drew near the Lord,
And saw his glory shine;
And when I read his holy word,
I called each promise mine.

4 But now, when evening shade prevails,
My soul in darkness mourns;
And when the morn the light reveals,
No light to me returns.

5 Rise, Lord, and help me to prevail;
O make my soul thy care;
I know thy mercy cannot fail;—
Let me that mercy share.

The promised blessing.

1 See, Jesus, thy disciples see;
The promised blessing give;
Met in thy name, we look to thee,
Expecting to receive.

2 Thee we expect, our faithful Lord,
Who in thy name are joined;
We wait, according to thy word,
Thee in the midst to find.

3 With us thou art assembled here,
But O, thyself reveal;
Son of the living God, appear!
Let us thy presence feel.

4 Breathe on us, Lord, in this our day,
And these dry bones shall live;
Speak peace into our hearts, and say,
The Holy Ghost receive.

5 Whom now we seek, O may we meet,
Jesus, the crucified;
Show us thy bleeding hands and feet,
Thou who for us hast died.

ST. MARTIN'S. C. M.

TANSUR. 1735.

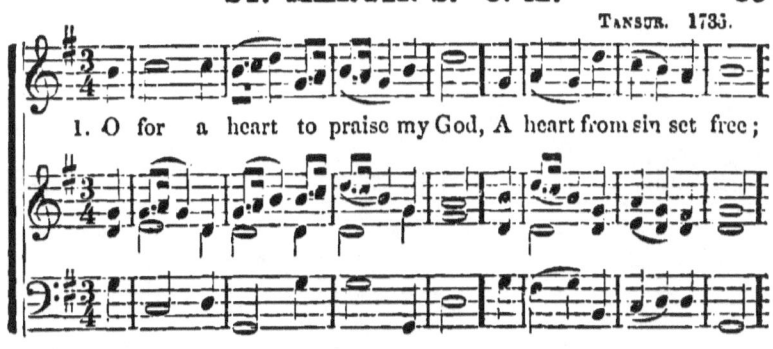

1. O for a heart to praise my God, A heart from sin set free;

A heart that always feels thy blood, So free - ly spilt for me

A perfect heart.

2 A heart resigned, submissive, meek,
 My great Redeemer's throne;
 Where only Christ is heard to speak,—
 Where Jesus reigns alone.

3 O for a lowly, contrite heart,
 Believing, true, and clean;
 Which neither life nor death can part
 From Him that dwells within:—

 A heart in every thought renewed,
 And full of love divine;
 Perfect, and right, and pure, and good,
 A copy, Lord, of thine.

5 Thy nature, gracious Lord, impart;
 Come quickly from above;
 Write thy new name upon my heart,—
 Thy new, best name of Love.

Entire purification.

1 Forever here my rest shall be,
 Close to thy bleeding side;
 This all my hope, and all my plea,
 For me the Saviour died.

2 My dying Saviour, and my God,
 Fountain for guilt and sin,
 Sprinkle me ever with thy blood,
 And cleanse and keep me clean.

3 Wash me, and make me thus thine own
 Wash me, and mine thou art;
 Wash me, but not my feet alone,—
 My hands, my head, my heart.

4 The' atonement of thy blood apply,
 Till faith to sight improve;
 Till hope in full fruition die,
 And all my soul be love.

ANTIOCH. C. M.

Dr. L. Mason. By permission.

1. Hark, the glad sound! the Saviour comes, The Saviour, promised long;
Let eve-ry heart prepare a throne, And every voice a song, And eve-ry voice a song,............ And eve-ry voice a song.

The Saviour comes.

2 He comes, the pris'ner to release,
In Satan's bondage held;
The gates of brass before him burst,
The iron fetters yield.

3 He comes, from thickest films of vice
To clear the mental ray,
And on the eyes oppressed with night,
To pour celestial day.

4 He comes, the broken heart to bind,
The wounded soul to cure,
And with the treasures of his grace,
T' enrich the humble poor.

The dear Name.

1 Jesus, the name high over all,
In hell, or earth, or sky;
Angels and men before it fall,
And devils fear and fly.

2 Jesus, the name to sinners dear,—
The name to sinners given;
It scatters all their guilty fear;
It turns their hell to heaven.

3 Oh, that the world might taste and see
The riches of his grace!
The arms of love that compass me,
Would all mankind embrace.

JOYFUL SOUND. C. M. Double.

E. L. WHITE.

1. O joyful sound of gospel grace, Christ shall in me appear!
I, e-ven I, shall see his face,—I shall be ho-ly here.
D. S. Conqueror thro' him, I soon shall seize, And wear it as my due.

The glorious crown of righteousness To me reached out I view;

A hope full of immortality.

The promised land, from Pisgah's top,
  I now exult to see:
My hope is full, (O, glorious hope!)
  Of immortality.
With me, I know, I feel, thou art;
  But this cannot suffice,
Unless thou plantest in my heart
  A constant paradise.

3 My earth thou waterest from on high,
  But make it all a pool:
Spring up, O Well, I ever cry;
  Spring up within my soul.
Come, O my God, thyself reveal;
  Fill all this mighty void:
Thou only canst my spirit fill;
  Come, O my God. my God.

MAN THE LIFE-BOAT. 8s & 7s.

J. W. D.

NO PARTING THERE. S. M.

J. W. D.

1. And may I still get there? Still reach the heavenly shore? The land for-ev-er bright and fair, Where sorrow reigns no more?

Cho. There'll be no parting there, There'll be no parting there; In heaven a-lone no sorrow's known, There'll be no parting there.

2 Shall I, unworthy I,
 To fear and doubting given,
Mount up at last, and happy fly
 On angel's wings to heaven. Cho.

3 Hail, love divine and pure!
 Hail, mercy from the skies!
My hopes are bright and now secure,
 Upborne by faith I rise. Cho.

4 I part with earth and sin,
 And shout the danger's past;
My Saviour takes me fully in,
 And I am his at last. W. HUNTER.

Conclusion of hymn on opposite page.

2 Courage! courage! she's in safety!
 See again her buoyant form,
By his gracious hand uplifted,
 Who controls the raging storm.
With her precious cargo freighted,
 Now the life-boat nears the shore;
Parents, brethren, friends, embracing,
 Those they thought to see no more.

3 Christian! pause, and deeply ponder;
 Is there nothing you can do?
The sinking ship, the storm, the life-boat,
 Have they not a voice for you?

There's a storm, a fearful tempest—
 Souls are sinking in despair;
There's a shore of blessed refuge,
 Try, O try to guide them there.

4 O, remember Him who saved you,
 Whose right hand deliverance wrought,
Who, from depths of guilt and anguish,
 You to peace and safety brought;
'Tis His voice who cheers you onward;
 "He that winneth souls is wise;"
Launch the Gospel's blessed life-boat;
 Venture all to win the prize.

SHIRLAND. S. M.

Stanley.

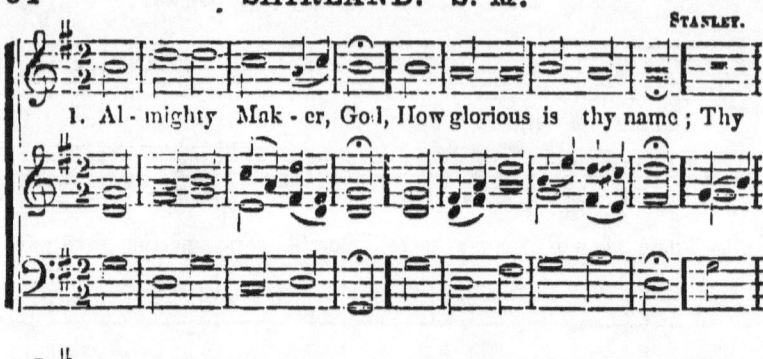

His name is glorious.

2 The lark mounts up the sky,
   With unambitious song;
   And bears her Maker's praise on high,
   Upon her artless tongue.

3 Fain would I rise and sing
   To my Creator too;
   Fain would my heart adore my King,
   And give him praises due.

4 Let joy and worship spend
   The remnant of my days:
   And to my God my soul ascend,
   In sweet perfumes of praise.

Blessings sought in prayer.

1 Behold the throne of grace!
   The promise calls me near;
   There Jesus shows a smiling face,
   And waits to answer prayer.

2 Thine image, Lord, bestow,
   Thy presence and thy love;
   I ask to serve thee here below,
   And reign with thee above.

3 Teach me to live by faith;
   Conform my will to thine;
   Let me victorious be in death,
   And then in glory shine.

4 If thou these blessings give,
   And wilt my portion be,
   All worldly joys I'll cheerful leave,
   And find my heaven in thee.

The Redeemer's tears.

1 Did Christ o'er sinners weep,
   And shall our cheeks be dry?
   Let floods of penitential grief
   Burst forth from every eye.

2 The Son of God in tears
   The wond'ring angels see;
   Be thou astonished, O my soul
   He shed those tears for thee.

3 He wept that we might weep;
   Each sin demands a tear:
   In heaven alone no sin is found,
   And there's no weeping there.

NEWTON. 8s.

1. How tedious and tasteless the hours, When Jesus no longer I see;
Sweet prospects, sweet birds and sweet flowers, Have lost all their sweetness to me
D.S. But when I am happy in him, December's as pleasant as May.
The mid-summer sun shines but dim, The fields strive in vain to look gay

2 His name yields the richest perfume,
And sweeter than music his voice;
His presence disperses my gloom,
And makes all within me rejoice:
I should, were he always thus nigh,
Have nothing to wish or to fear;
No mortal so happy as I,
My summer would last all the year.

3 Content with beholding his face,
My all to his pleasure resigned;
No changes of season or place
Would make any change in my mind;

While blessed with a sense of his love,
A palace a toy would appear;
And prisons would palaces prove,
If Jesus would dwell with me there.

4 Dear Lord, if indeed I am thine,
If thou art my sun and my song;
Say, why do I languish and pine?
And why are my winters so long?
O, drive these dark clouds from my sky,
Thy soul-cheering presence restore;
Or take me to thee up on high,
Where winter and clouds are no more

HOPE IN JESUS. 8s & 6s.

Words by S. ADAMS WIGGIN.
GRATEFULLLY INSCRIBED TO REV. J. W. DADMUN.
J. W. D

1. Hope is the lovely budding flow'r, Of Faith's o'er-arching tree;
Hope is the waking of the pow'r, That sets the spirit free.
D.S. Hope is the light of life, without Our faith would droop and die.

Hope is the loss of eve-ry doubt, That clouds the inner eye;

2 Hope is the anchor of the soul,
   When clouds of sorrow rise;
Hope can pale death's fell power control,
   And raise us to the skies.
Hope is the "nimbus," rays divine,
   Round the Redeemer's head;
Which on our weary way may shine,
   And holy comfort shed.

3 Hope, wakened in the sinner's heart,
   Dispelleth all his fears;
Dawns on him now the better part,
   Hope wipes away his tears.
Hope is the Christian's life and stay;
   With "hope in Jesus" blest,
Our ransomed spirits soar away
   To everlasting rest.

HERE IS NO REST.

2 Here fierce temptations beset me around,
   Here is no rest, here is no rest.
   Here I am grieved while my foes me surround;
   Yet I am blest, I am blest.
   Let them revile me, and scoff at my name,
   Laugh at my weeping, endeavor to shame,
   I will go forward, for this is my theme,
      There, there is rest—there is rest.

3 Here are afflictions and trials severe;
   Here is no rest, here is no rest;
   Here I must part with the friends I hold dear,
      Yet I am blest, I am blest.
   Sweet is the promise I read in his word;
   Blessed are they who have died in the Lord;
   They have been called to receive their reward;
      There, there is rest—there is rest.

98. O, SING TO ME OF HEAVEN. S. M.

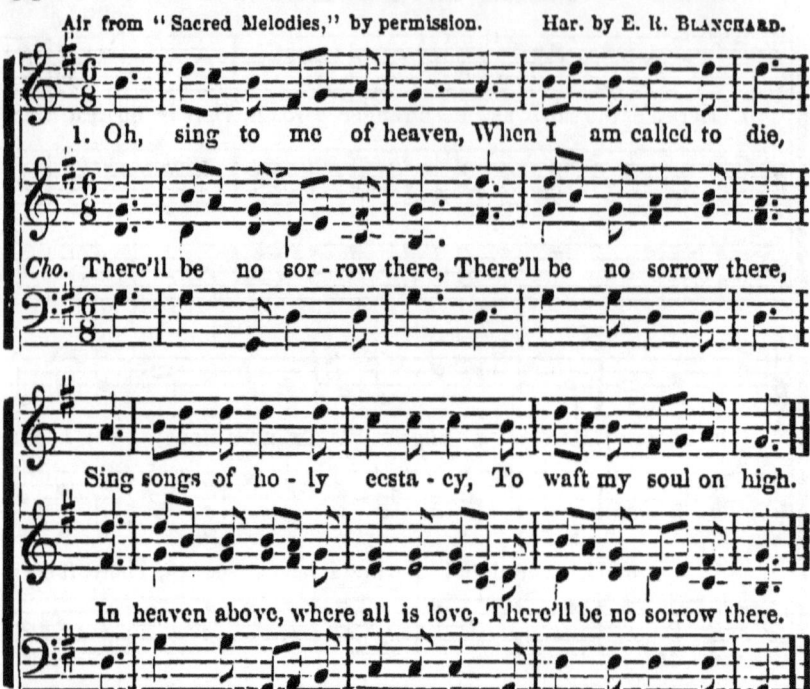

Air from "Sacred Melodies," by permission.   Har. by E. R. BLANCHARD.

1. Oh, sing to me of heaven, When I am called to die,

Cho. There'll be no sor-row there, There'll be no sorrow there,

Sing songs of ho-ly ecsta-cy, To waft my soul on high.

In heaven above, where all is love, There'll be no sorrow there.

2 When cold and sluggish drops
   Roll off my marble brow,
Break forth in songs of joyfulness,
   Let heaven begin below.

3 When the last moments come,
   O, watch my dying face,
To catch the bright seraphic gleam
   Which o'er my features plays.

4 Then to my raptured ear,
   Let one sweet song be given;
Let music charm me last on earth,
   And greet me first in heaven.

5 Then close my sightless eyes,
   And lay me down to rest;
And fold my pale and icy hands
   Upon my lifeless breast.

6 Then round my senseless clay
   Assemble those I love;
And sing of heaven, delightful heaven,
   My glorious home above.   MRS. DANA.

All-sufficient grace.

1 Grace! 'tis a charming sound,
   Harmonious to the ear;
Heaven with the echo shall resound,
   And all the earth shall hear.

CHO. I'm glad salvation's free,
   I'm glad salvation's free;
Salvation's free for you and me,
   I'm glad salvation's free.

2 Grace first contrived a way
   To save rebellious man;
And all the steps that grace display,
   Which drew the wondrous plan.

3 Grace taught my roving feet
   To tread the heavenly road;
And new supplies each hour I meet,
   While pressing on to God.

4 Grace all the work shall crown,
   Through everlasting days;
It lays in heaven the topmost stone,
   And well deserves our praise.

NUREMBURG. 7s.

GERMAN.

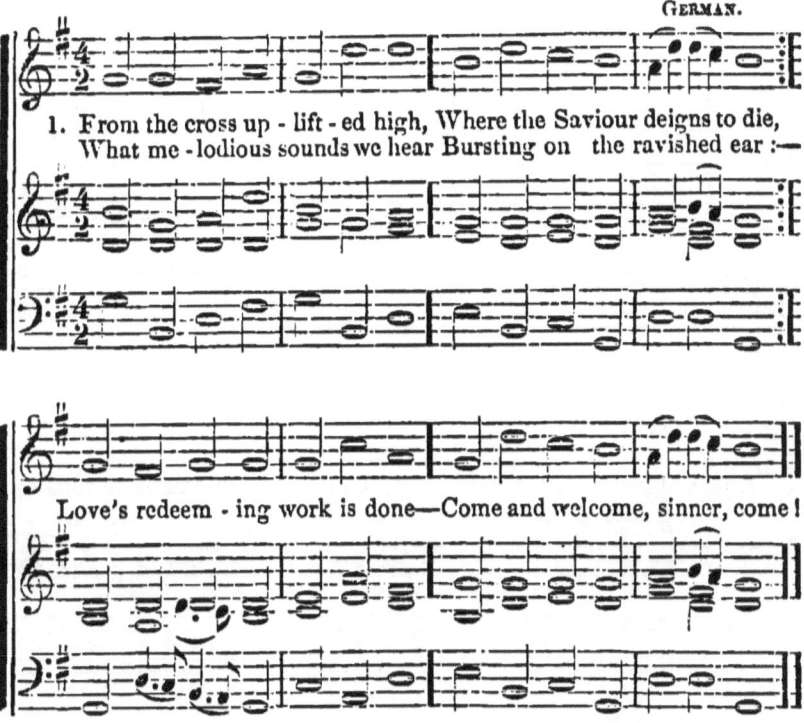

1. From the cross up-lift-ed high, Where the Saviour deigns to die, What me-lodious sounds we hear Bursting on the ravished ear:—
Love's redeem-ing work is done—Come and welcome, sinner, come!

Come, and welcome.

1 From the cross uplifted high,
Where the Saviour deigns to die,
What melodious sounds we hear
Bursting on the ravished ear:
Love's redeeming work is done—
Come and welcome, sinner, come!

2 Sprinkled now with blood the throne—
Why beneath thy burdens groan?
On his pierced body laid,
Justice owns the ransom paid;
Bow the knee,—embrace the Son—
Come and welcome, sinner, come!

3 Spread for thee, the festal board
See with richest bounty stored;
To thy Father's bosom pressed,
Thou shalt be a child confessed,
Never from his house to roam;
Come and welcome, sinner, come!

In Darkness.

1 Once I thought my mountain strong,
Firmly fixed, no more to move;
Then my Saviour was my song,
Then my soul was filled with love:
Those were happy, golden days,
Sweetly spent in prayer and praise.

2 Little, then, myself I knew,
Little thought of Satan's power;
Now I feel my sins renew,
Now I feel the stormy hour;
Sin has put my joys to flight,—
Sin has turned my day to night.

3 Saviour! shine, and cheer my soul
Did my dying hopes revive;
Make my wounded spirit whole,
Far away the tempter drive;
Speak the word and set me free
Let me live alone to thee.

AMSTERDAM. 7s & 6s.

1. Rise, my soul, and stretch thy wings, Thy bet-ter portion trace;
Rise from transi - to - ry things Toward heaven, thy native place;
Sun, and moon, and stars de - cay; Time shall soon this earth remove;
Rise, my soul, and haste a - way To seats prepared a - bove.

The better portion.

2 Rivers to the ocean run,
  Nor stay in all their course;
Fire, ascending, seeks the sun;
  Both speed them to their source:
So a soul that's born of God,
  Pants to view his glorious face;
Upward tends to his abode,
  To rest in his embrace.

3 Cease, ye pilgrims, cease to mourn;
  Press onward to the prize;
Soon our Saviour will return
  Triumphant in the skies:
There we'll join the heavenly train,
  Welcomed to partake the bliss;
Fly from sorrow, care, and pain,
  To realms of endless peace.

BEAUTIFUL ZION. 101

From the "Musical Pioneer," by permission.   S. J VAIL.

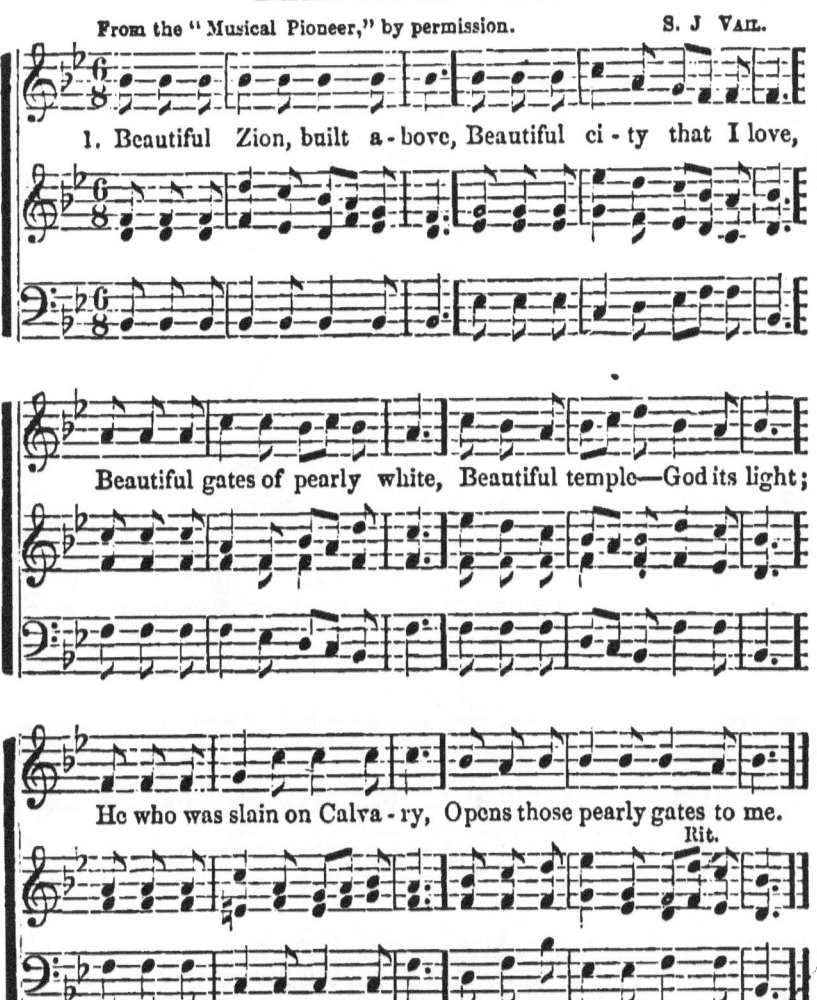

1. Beautiful Zion, built above, Beautiful city that I love,
Beautiful gates of pearly white, Beautiful temple—God its light;
He who was slain on Calvary, Opens those pearly gates to me.

2 Beautiful heaven, where all is light,
Beautiful angels clothed in white,
Beautiful strains that never tire,
Beautiful harps through all the choir;
There shall I join the chorus sweet,
Worshiping at the Saviour's feet.

3 Beautiful crowns on every brow,
Beautiful palms the conquerors show,
Beautiful robes the ransomed wear,
Beautiful all who enter there;
Thither I press with eager feet,
There shall my rest be long and sweet.

4 Beautiful throne of Christ our King,
Beautiful songs the angels sing;
Beautiful rest, all wanderings cease,
Beautiful home of perfect peace;
There shall my eyes the Saviour see,
Haste to this heavenly home with me.

DUNDEE. C. M.

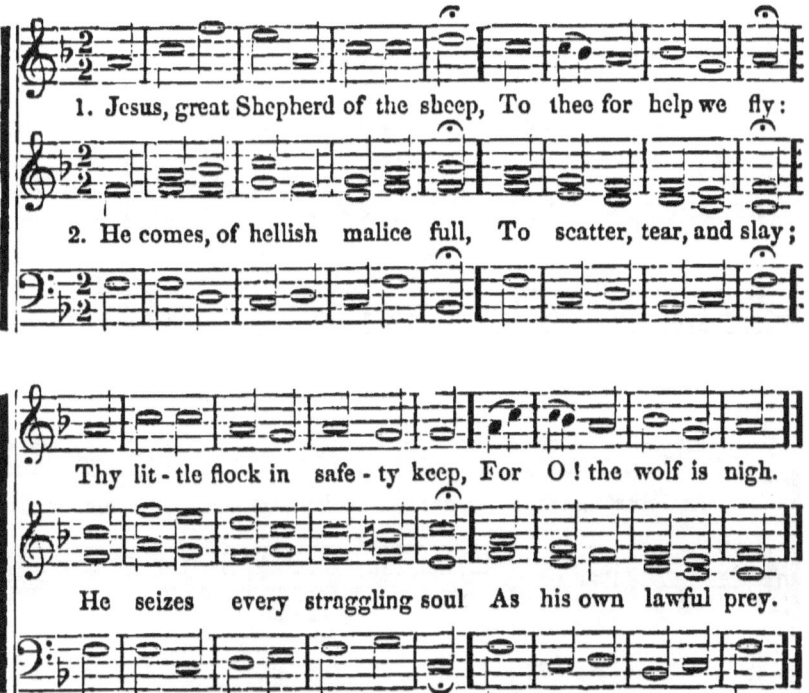

1. Jesus, great Shepherd of the sheep, To thee for help we fly:
Thy lit-tle flock in safe-ty keep, For O! the wolf is nigh.

2. He comes, of hellish malice full, To scatter, tear, and slay;
He seizes every straggling soul As his own lawful prey.

Safety in union.

3 Us into thy protection take,
And gather with thine arm;
Unless the fold we first forsake,
The wolf can never harm.

4 We laugh to scorn his cruel power,
While by our Shepherd's side;
The sheep he never can devour,
Unless he first divide.

5 O, do not suffer him to part
The souls that here agree;
But make us of one mind and heart,
And keep us one in thee.

6 Together let us sweetly live,—
Together let us die;
And each a starry crown receive,
And reign above the sky.

Conclusion of hymn on opposite page.

2 I heard the voice of Jesus say,
Behold, I freely give
The living water; thirsty one,
Stoop down and drink, and live.
I came to Jesus, and I drank
Of that life-giving stream;
My thirst was quenched, my soul revived,
And now I live in him.

3 I heard the voice of Jesus say,
I am this dark world's light;
Look unto me, thy morn shall rise
And all thy day be bright.
I looked to Jesus, and I found
In him my Star, my Sun;
And in that light of life I'll walk
'Till travelling days are done.

WARD. L. M.

From a Scotch tune, by L. MASON. By permission.

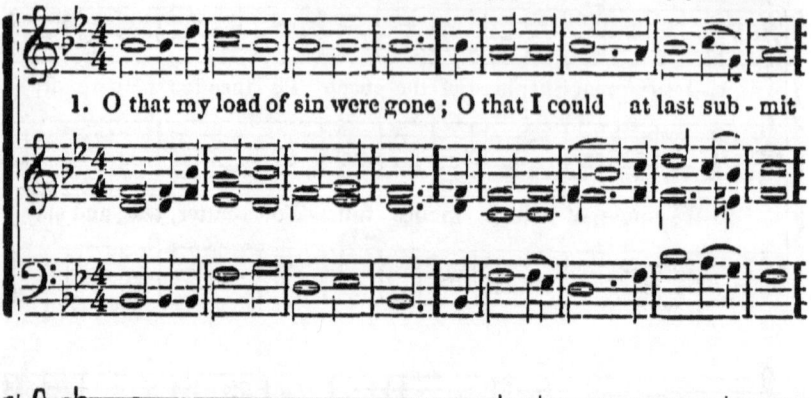

1. O that my load of sin were gone; O that I could at last sub-mit

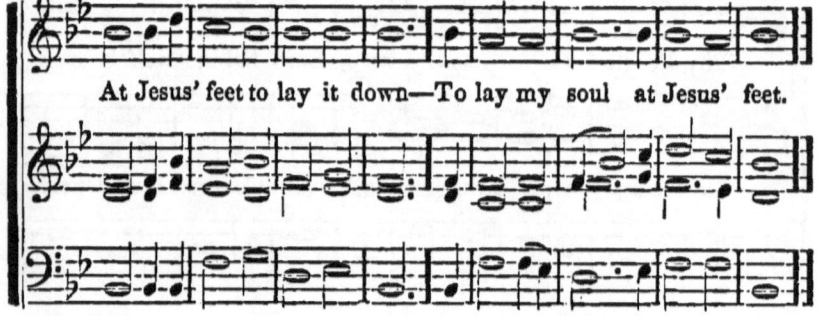

At Jesus' feet to lay it down—To lay my soul at Jesus' feet.

2 Rest for my soul I long to find:
  Saviour of all, if mine thou art,
  Give me thy meek and lowly mind,
  And stamp thine image on my heart.

3 Break off the yoke of inbred sin,
  And fully set my spirit free;
  I cannot rest till pure within,—
  Till I am wholly lost in thee.

4 Fain would I learn of thee, my God;
  Thy light and easy burden prove;
  The cross all stained with hallowed blood,
  The labor of thy dying love.

5 I would, but thou must give the power;
  My heart from every sin release;
  Bring near, bring near the joyful hour,
  And fill me with thy perfect peace.

The divine Teacher.

1 How sweetly flowed the gospel's sound
  From lips of gentleness and grace,
  While list'ning thousands gathered round,
  And joy and reverence filled the place.

  From heaven he came, of heaven he spoke,
  To heaven he led his followers' way;
  Dark clouds of gloomy night he broke,
  Unveiling an immortal day.

3 Come, wanderers, to my Father's home;
  Come, all ye weary ones, and rest.
  Yes, sacred Teacher! we will come,
  Obey, and be forever blest.

4 Decay, then, tenements of dust!
  Pillars of earthly pride, decay!
  A nobler mansion waits the just,
  And Jesus has prepared the way.

HAPPY DAY. L. M.

From "Wesleyan Sacred Harp."

1. O happy day that fixed my choice On thee, my Savior and my God! Well may this glowing heart rejoice, And tell its raptures all abroad.

Happy day, happy day, when Jesus washed my sins a-way;

He taught me how to watch and pray, And live re-joicing every day,

2 O happy bond, that seals my vows
To Him who merits all my love;
Let cheerful anthems fill his house,
While to that sacred shrine I move.

3 'Tis done, the great transaction's done;
I am my Lord's, and he is mine;
He drew me, and I followed on,
Charmed to confess the voice divine.

4 Now rest, my long-divided heart;
Fixed on this blissful centre, rest;
Nor ever from thy Lord depart;
With him of every good possessed.

5 High heaven, that heard the solemn vow,
That vow renewed shall daily hear,
Till in life's latest hour I bow,
And bless in death a bond so dear.

HEBRON. L. M.

Dr. Lowell Mason. By permission.

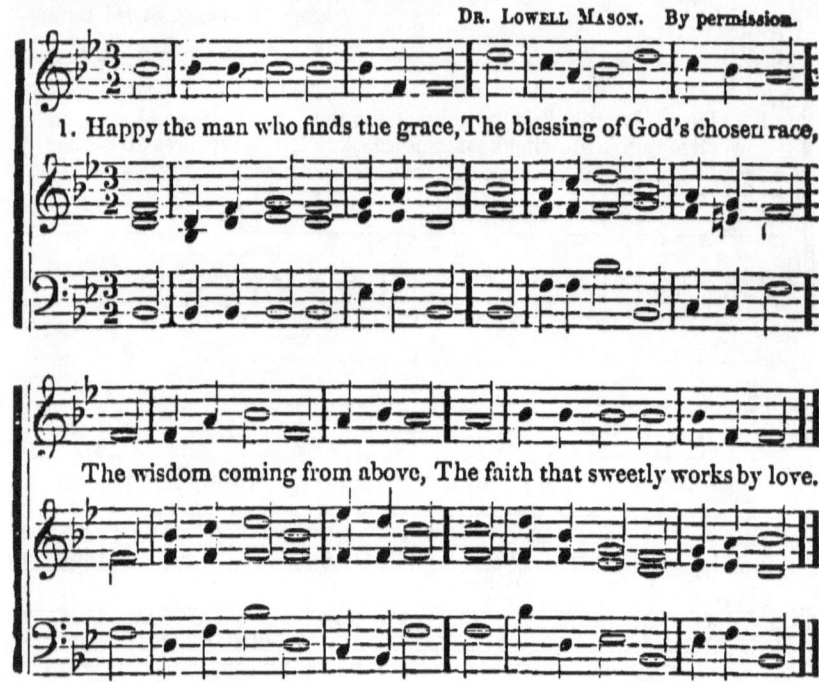

1. Happy the man who finds the grace, The blessing of God's chosen race, The wisdom coming from above, The faith that sweetly works by love.

The unspeakable gift.

2 Happy, beyond description, he
Who knows the Saviour died for me!
The gift unspeakable obtains,
And heavenly understanding gains.

3 Wisdom divine! who tells the price
Of wisdom's costly merchandise?
Wisdom to silver we prefer,
And gold is dross compared to her.

4 Her hands are filled with length of days,
True riches, and immortal praise,—
Riches of Christ on all bestowed,
And honor that descends from God.

5 To purest joys she all invites,—
Chaste, holy, spiritual delights;
Her ways are ways of pleasantness,
And all her flowery paths are peace.

6 Happy the man who wisdom gains;
Thrice happy, who his guest retains:
He owns, and shall forever own,
Wisdom, and Christ, and heaven are one.

Love that passeth knowledge.

1 Of Him who did salvation bring,
I could forever think and sing;
Arise, ye needy,—he'll relieve;
Arise, ye guilty,—he'll forgive.

2 Ask but his grace, and lo, 'tis given;
Ask, and he turns your hell to heaven:
Though sin and sorrow wound my soul,
Jesus, thy balm will make it whole.

3 To shame our sins he blushed in blood;
He closed his eyes to show us God:
Let all the world fall down and know,
That none but God such love can show.

4 'Tis thee I love, for thee alone
I shed my tears and make my moan;
Where'er I am, where'er I move,
I meet the object of my love.

5 Insatiate to this spring I fly;
I drink, and yet am ever dry;
Ah! who against thy charms is proof?
Ah! who that loves, can love enough?

COWPER. C. M. 107

L. Mason. By permission.

1. This is the day the Lord hath made; O earth, rejoice and sing;
Let songs of triumph hail the morn; Hosanna to our King,
Hosanna to our King!

2 The Stone the builders set at naught,
That Stone has now become
The sure foundation, and the strength
Of Zion's heavenly dome.

3 Christ is that stone, rejected once,
And numbered with the slain;
Now raised in glory, o'er his Church
Eternally to reign.

4 This is the day the Lord hath made;
O earth, rejoice and sing:
With songs of triumph hail the morn;
Hosanna to our King!

The Resolution.

1 Come, humble sinner, in whose breast
A thousand thoughts revolve;
Come, with your guilt and fear oppressed,
And make this last resolve:—

2 I'll go to Jesus, though my sin
Like mountains round me close;
I know his courts, I'll enter in,
Whatever may oppose.

3 Prostrate I'll lie before his throne,
And there my guilt confess;

I'll tell him I'm a wretch undone,
Without his sovereign grace.

4 Perhaps he will admit my plea,
Perhaps will hear my prayer;
But, if I perish, I will pray,
And perish only there.

5 I can but perish if I go;
I am resolved to try;
For if I stay away, I know
I must forever die.

2 Look, how we grovel here below,
 Fond of these earthly toys;
 Our souls, how heavily they go,
 To reach eternal joys.

3 In vain we tune our formal songs,—
 In vain we strive to rise;
 Hosannas languish on our tongues,
 And our devotion dies.

4 Father, and shall we ever live
 At this poor, dying rate;
 Our love so faint, so cold to thee,
 And thine to us so great?

5 Come, Holy Spirit, heavenly Dove,
 With all thy quick'ning powers;
 Come, shed abroad a Saviour's love,
 And that shall kindle ours.

TURNER, Concluded.   109

Saviour's love, And that shall kin-dle ours.

Triumphant joy.

1 My God, the spring of all my joys,
　The life of my delights,
　The glory of my brightest days,
　And comfort of my nights:

2 In darkest shades, if thou appear,
　My dawning is begun;
　Thou art my soul's bright morning star,
　And thou my rising sun.

3 The opening heavens around me shine
　With beams of sacred bliss.

　If Jesus shows his mercy mine,
　And whispers I am his.

4 My soul would leave this heavy clay,
　At that transporting word;
　Run up with joy the shining way,
　To see and praise my Lord.

5 Fearless of hell and ghastly death,
　I'd break through every foe;
　The wings of love and arms of faith
　Would bear me conqueror through.

SICILY. 8s & 7s.

1. Lord, dismiss us with thy blessing, Fill our hearts with joy and peace;
Let us each thy love possessing, Triumph in redeeming grace;
O refresh us, O refresh us, Trav'ling thro' this wilderness.

For the fulness of peace and joy.

2 Thanks we give, and adoration,
　For thy gospel's joyful sound;
　May the fruits of thy salvation,

　In our hearts and lives abound;
　May thy presence
　With us evermore be found.

AZMON. C. M.

Arranged from GLASER, by L. MASON. By permission

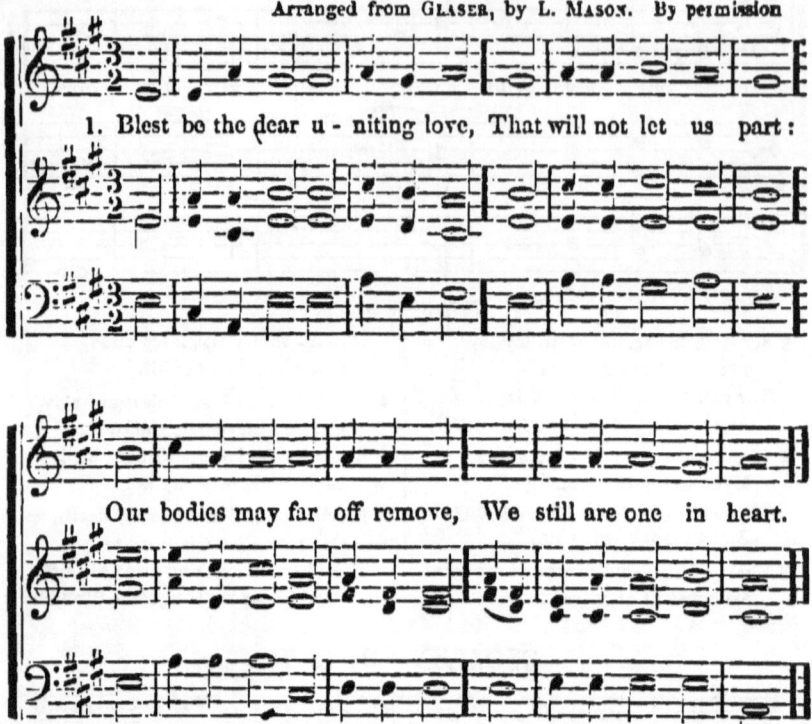

1. Blest be the dear u-niting love, That will not let us part: Our bodies may far off remove, We still are one in heart.

United, though separated.

2 Joined in one spirit to our Head,
   Where he appoints, we go;
   And still in Jesus' footsteps tread,
   And show his praise below.

3 O may we ever walk in him,
   And nothing know beside,—
   Nothing desire, nothing esteem,
   But Jesus crucified.

4 Closer and closer let us cleave
   To his beloved embrace;
   Expect his fulness to receive,
   And grace to answer grace.

5 Partakers of the Saviour's grace,
   The same in mind and heart,
   Nor joy, nor grief, nor time, nor place,
   Nor life, nor death can part.

Behold the Lamb.

1 Look unto Christ, ye nations; own
   Your God, ye fallen race;
   Look, and be saved through faith alone,
   Be justified by grace.

2 See all your sins on Jesus laid:
   The Lamb of God was slain;
   His soul was once an offering made
   For every soul of man.

3 Awake from guilty nature's sleep,
   And Christ shall give you light;
   Cast all your sins into the deep,
   And wash the Ethiop white.

4 With me, your chief, ye then shall know,
   Shall feel your sins forgiven;
   Anticipate your heaven below,
   And own that love is heaven.

GANGES. C. P. M.

1. How happy is the pilgrim's lot, How free from every anxious thought,
From worldly hope and fear! Confined to neither court nor cell, His
soul disdains on earth to dwell,
He only sojourns here.

The pilgrim's happy lot.

2 This happiness in part is mine,
Already saved from low design,
From every creature love;
Blest with the scorn of finite good,
My soul is lightened of its load,
And seeks the things above.

3 There is my house and portion fair;
My treasure and my heart are there,
And my abiding home;
For me my elder brethren stay,
And angels beckon me away,
And Jesus bids me come

4 I come, thy servant, Lord, replies;
I come to meet thee in the skies,
And claim my heavenly rest!
Soon will the pilgrim's journey end;
Then, O my Saviour, Brother, Friend,
Receive me to thy breast!

Bliss-inspiring hope.

1 Come on, my partners in distress,
My comrades through the wilderness,
Who still your bodies feel:
Awhile forget your griefs and fears,
And look beyond this vale of tears,
To that celestial hill.

2 Beyond the bounds of time and space,
Look forward to that heavenly place,
The saints' secure abode;
On faith's strong eagle pinions rise,
And force your passage to the skies,
And scale the mount of God.

3 Who suffer with our Master here,
We shall before his face appear,
And by his side sit down :
To patient faith the prize is sure;
And all that to the end endure
The cross, shall wear the crown.

ROCKINGHAM. L. M.

Dr. Lowell Mason. By permission.

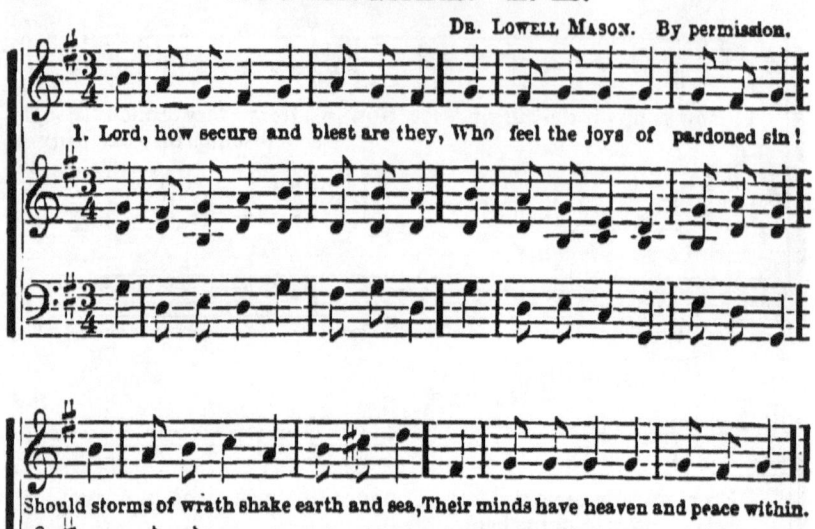

1. Lord, how secure and blest are they, Who feel the joys of pardoned sin! Should storms of wrath shake earth and sea, Their minds have heaven and peace within.

The bliss of assurance.

2 The day glides sweetly o'er their heads,
  Made up of innocence and love;
  And soft, and silent as the shades,
  Their nightly minutes gently move.

Quick as their thoughts their joys come on,
  But fly not half so swift away;
  Their souls are ever bright as noon,
  And calm as summer evenings be.

4 How oft they look to th' heavenly hills,
  Where groves of living pleasure grow;
  And longing hopes, and cheerful smiles,
  Sit undisturbed upon their brow.

5 They scorn to seek our golden toys,
  But spend the day, and share the night,
  In numbering o'er the richer joys
  That heaven prepares for their delight.

Design of Prayer.

1 Prayer is appointed to convey
  The blessings God designs to give:
  Long as they live should Christians pray;
  They learn to pray when first they live.

2 If pain afflict, or wrongs oppress;
  If cares distract, or fears dismay;
  If guilt deject; if sin distress,
  In every case, still watch and pray.

'Tis prayer supports the soul that's weak;
  Tho' thought be broken, language lame,
  Pray, if thou canst or canst not speak;
  But pray with faith in Jesus' name.

4 Depend on him; thou canst not fail;
  Make all thy wants and wishes known;
  Fear not; his merits must prevail;
  Ask but in faith, it shall be done.

LISBON. S. M.

J. READ.

1. And can I yet de-lay My lit-tle all to give?

To tear my soul from earth a-way For Jesus to receive?

2 Nay, but I yield, I yield;
 I can hold out no more:
 I sink, by dying love compelled,
 And own thee conqueror.

3 Though late, I all forsake;
 My friends, my all, resign:
 Gracious Redeemer, take, O take,
 And seal me ever thine.

4 Come, and possess me whole,
 Nor hence again remove;
 Settle and fix my wavering soul
 With all thy weight of love.

5 My one desire be this,—
 Thy only love to know;
 To seek and taste no other bliss,
 No other good below.

6 My life, my portion thou,
 Thou all-sufficient art:

My hope, my heavenly treasure, now
 Enter, and keep my heart.

Accepting the invitation.

1 Come, weary sinners, come,
 Groaning beneath your load;
 The Saviour calls his wanderers home
 Haste to your pardoning God

2 Come, all by guilt oppressed,
 Answer the Saviour's call—
 O come, and I will give you rest,
 And I will save you all.

3 Redeemer, full of love,
 We would thy word obey,
 And all thy faithful merc'es prove:
 O take our guilt away.

4 We would on thee rely;
 On thee would cast our care;
 Now to thine arms of mercy fly,
 And find salvation there.

WELTON. L. M.

Arranged from Rev. C. Malan, by L. Mason. By permission

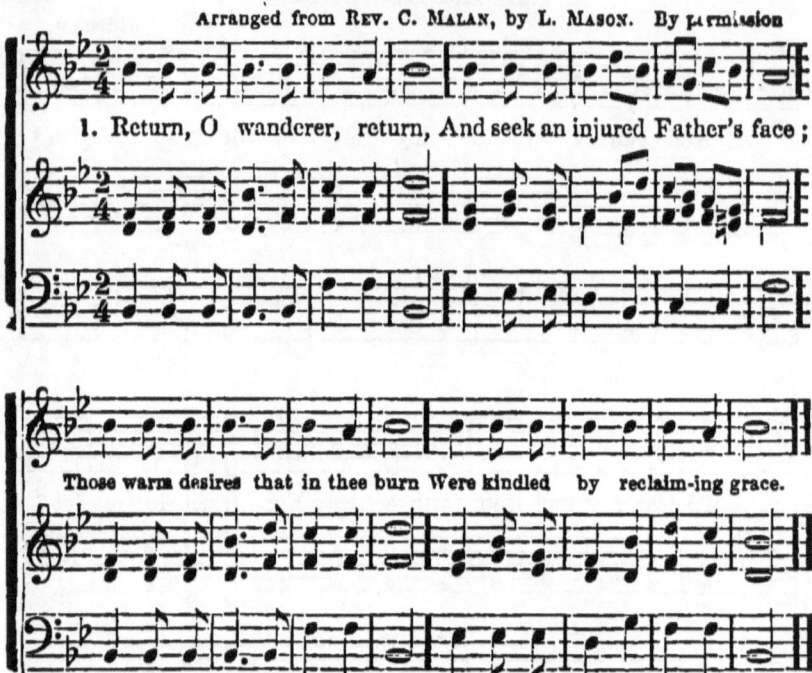

1. Return, O wanderer, return, And seek an injured Father's face; Those warm desires that in thee burn Were kindled by reclaim-ing grace.

The wanderer recalled.

2 Return, O wanderer, return,
And seek a Father's melting heart,
Whose pitying eyes thy grief discern,
Whose hand can heal thine inward smart.

3 Return, O wanderer, return;
He heard thy deep, repentant sigh:
He saw thy softened spirit mourn,
When no intruding tear was nigh

4 Return, O wanderer, return,
Thy Saviour bids thy spirit live;
Go to his bleeding feet, and learn
How freely Jesus can forgive.

5 Return, O wanderer, return,
And wipe away thy falling tear;
'Tis God who says—"no longer mourn,"
'Tis mercy's voice invites thee near.

6 Return, O wanderer, return,
Regain thy lost lamented rest;
Jehovah's melting bowels yearn,
To clasp the wanderer to his breast.

Meekness and patience.

1 Thou Lamb of God, thou Prince of peace,
For thee my thirsty soul doth pine;
My longing heart implores thy grace;
O make me in thy likeness shine.

2 With fraudless, even, humble mind,
Thy will in all things may I see;
In love be every wish resigned,
And hallowed my whole heart to thee.

3 When pain o'er my weak flesh prevails,
With lamb-like patience arm my breast;
When grief my wounded soul assails,
In lowly meekness may I rest.

4 Close by thy side still may I keep,
Howe'er life's various current flow;
With steadfast eye mark every step,
And follow where my Lord doth go.

5 Thou, Lord, the dreadful fight hast won;
Alone thou hast the wine-press trod;
In me thy strengthening grace be shown;
O may I conquer through thy blood.

WOODLAND. C. M. 115

NATIONAL CHURCH HARMONY.

1. Lovers of pleasure more than God, For you he suffered pain; For you the Saviour spilt his blood, For you the Saviour spilt his blood: And shall he bleed in vain?

2 Sinners, his life for you he paid;
Your basest crimes he bore;
Your sins were all on Jesus laid,
That you might sin no more.

3 To earth the great Redeemer came,
That you may come to heaven;
Believe, believe in Jesus' name,
And all your sin's forgiven.

Perfect freedom.

1 If thou impart thyself to me,
No other good I need:
If thou the Son, shalt make me free,
I shall be free indeed.

2 I cannot rest till in thy blood
I full redemption have;
But thou, through whom I come to God,
Canst to the utmost save.

3 From sin,—the guilt, the power, the [pain,
Thou wilt redeem my soul:
Lord, I believe—and not in vain;
My faith shall make me whole.

4 I, too, with thee, shall walk in white;
With all thy saints shall prove
The length and depth, and breadth and
Of everlasting love.   [height,

BOYLSTON. S. M.

Dr. Lowell Mason. By permission.

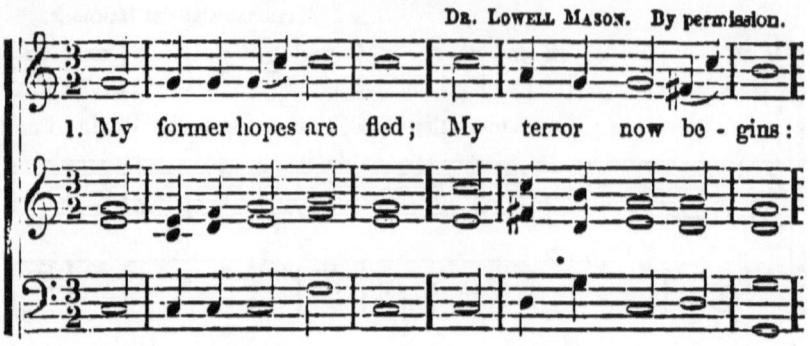

1. My former hopes are fled; My terror now be-gins:

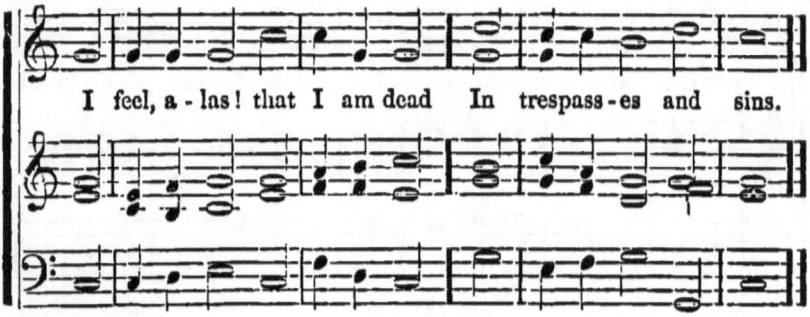

I feel, a-las! that I am dead In trespass-es and sins.

154 *The Day-star from on high.*

2 Ah, whither shall I fly?
   I hear the thunder roar:
The law proclaims destruction nigh,
   And vengeance at the door.

3 When I review my ways,
   I dread impending doom:
But, hark! a friendly whisper says,—
   Flee from the wrath to come.

4 With trembling hope, I see
   A glimm'ring from afar;
A beam of day that shines for me,
   To save me from despair.

5 Forerunner of the sun,
   It marks the pilgrim's way;
I'll gaze upon it while I run,
   And watch the rising day.

155 *Sow beside all waters.*

1 Sow in the morn thy seed;
   At eve hold not thy hand;
To doubt and fear give thou no heed,—
   Broad-cast it o'er the land.

2 Thou know'st not which shall thrive,—
   The late or early sown;
Grace keeps the precious germ alive,
   When and wherever strown:

3 And duly shall appear,
   In verdure, beauty, strength,
The tender blade, the stalk, the ear,
   And the full corn at length.

4 Thou canst not toil in vain:
   Cold, heat, and moist, and dry,
Shall foster and mature the grain
   For garners in the sky.

BRIDGEWATER. L. M.

EDSON. 1784.

2 Might I enjoy the meanest place
Within thy house, O God of grace,
Not tents of ease, or thrones of power,
Should tempt my feet to leave thy door.

3 God is our sun, he makes our day;
God is our shield, he guards our way
From all assaults of hell and sin,
From foes without, and foes within.

4 All needful grace will God bestow,
And crown that grace with glory too:
He gives us all things, and withholds
No real good from upright souls.

5 O God our King, whose sov'reign sway
The glorious hosts of heaven obey,
And devils at thy presence flee,
Blest is the man that trusts in thee

UXBRIDGE. L. M.

L. Mason. By permission.

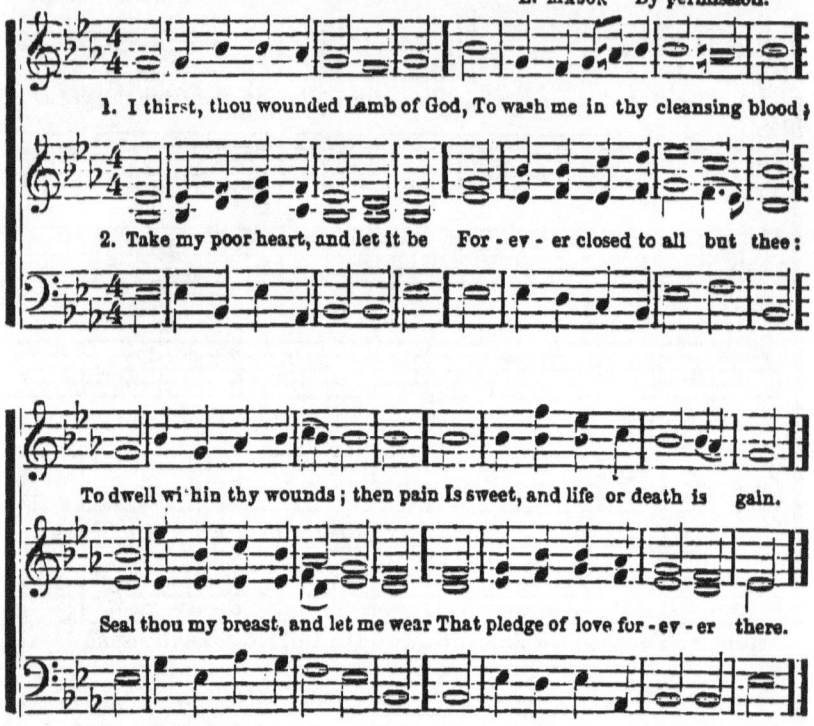

1. I thirst, thou wounded Lamb of God, To wash me in thy cleansing blood;
   To dwell within thy wounds; then pain Is sweet, and life or death is gain.

2. Take my poor heart, and let it be For-ev-er closed to all but thee:
   Seal thou my breast, and let me wear That pledge of love for-ev-er there.

3 How blest are they who still abide
Close sheltered in thy bleeding side!
Who thence their life and strength derive,
And by thee move, and in thee live.

4 What are our works but sin and death,
Till thou thy quickening Spirit breathe?
Thou giv'st the power thy grace to move;
O wondrous grace! O boundless love!

5 How can it be, thou heavenly King,
That thou shouldst us to glory bring;
Make slaves the partners of thy throne,
Decked with a never-fading crown?

6 Hence our hearts melt, our eyes o'erflow,
Our words are lost, nor will we know,
Nor will we think of aught beside,—
My Lord, my Love, is crucified.

Filial confidence and joy.

1 Great God, indulge my humble claim;
  Be thou my hope, my joy, my rest;
The glories that compose thy name
  Stand all engaged to make me blest.

2 Thou great and good, thou just and wise,
  Thou art my Father and my God;
And I am thine by sacred ties,—
  Thy son, thy servant bought with blood.

3 With heart and eyes, and lifted hands,
  For thee I long, to thee I look;
As travellers in thirsty lands
  Pant for the cooling water brook.

4 I'll lift my hands, I'll raise my voice,
  While I have breath to pray or praise:
This work shall make my heart rejoice,
  And fill the remnant of my days,

ATONEMENT. 10s, 7s & 9s.

1. Saw ye my Saviour, saw ye my Saviour, Saw ye my Saviour and God! O, he died on Cal-va-ry, To a-tone for you and me, And to purchase our pardon with blood.
2. He was ex-tend-ed— he was ex-tend-ed, Painful-ly nailed to the cross: Here he bowed his head and died, Thus my Lord was cru-ci-fied, To a-tone for a world that was lost.

3 Jesus hung bleeding—Jesus hung bleeding
  Three dreadful hours in pain;
  And the solid rocks were rent
  Through creation's vast extent,
  When the Jews crucified the God-man.

4 Darkness prevailed—darkness prevailed,
  Darkness prevailed o'er the land,
  And the sun refused to shine,
  When his Majesty Divine,
  Was derided insulted, and slain.

5 When it was finished—when it was finished,
  And the atonement was made,
  He was taken by the great,
  And embalmed in spices sweet,
  And was in a new sepulchre laid.

6 Hail, mighty Saviour—hail, mighty Saviour,
  Prince, and the author of peace!
  O, he burst the bars of death,
  And, triumphant, from beneath,
  He ascended to mansions of bliss.

SABBATH MORN. 7s.

L. MASON. By permission.

1. Safely through a-nother week, God has brought us on our way; Let us now a blessing seek, Waiting in his courts to-day; Day of all the week the best; Emblem of e-ter-nal rest— Day of all the week the best; Emblem of e-ternal rest.

ZEPHYR. L. M.

W. B. Bradbury. By permission

1. Why should we start, and fear to die? What timorous worms we mortals are!

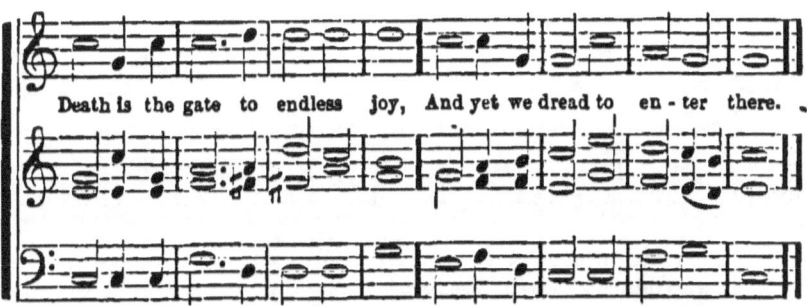

Death is the gate to endless joy, And yet we dread to en-ter there.

Christ's presence in death.

2 The pains, the groans, the dying strife,
  Fright our approaching souls away;
And we shrink back again to life,
  Fond of our prison and our clay.

3 O would my Lord his servant meet,
  My soul would stretch her wings in haste,
Fly fearless through death's iron gate,
  Nor feel the terrors as she passed.

4 Jesus can make a dying bed
  Feel soft as downy pillows are,
While on his breast I lean my head,
  And breathe my life out sweetly there

Conclusion of hymn on opposite page.

2 While we seek supplies of grace,
    Through the dear Redeemer's name,
  Show thy reconciling face—
    Take away our sin and shame:
  From our worldly cares set free,
    May we rest this day in thee.

3 Here we come thy name to praise;
    Let us feel thy presence near;
  May thy glory meet our eyes,
    While we in thy house appear,
  Here afford us, Lord, a taste
    Of our everlasting feast.

4 May the gospel's joyful sound,
    Conquer sinners, comfort saints;
  Make the fruits of grace abound,
    Bring relief from all complaints:
  Thus let all our Sabbaths prove,
    Till we join the church above.

MISSIONARY CHANT. L. M.

CH. ZEUNER. By permission.

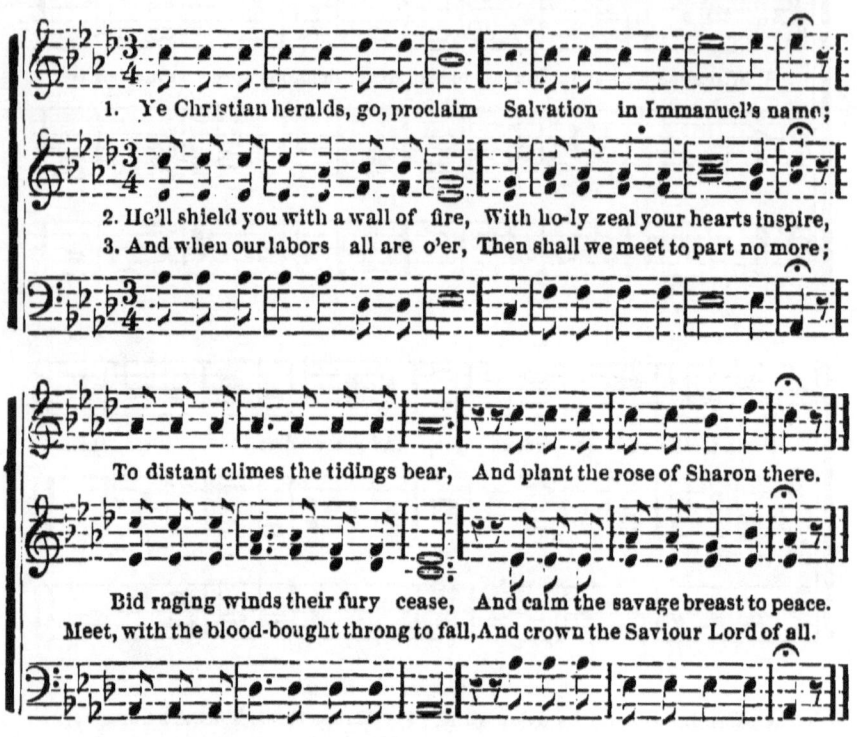

1. Ye Christian heralds, go, proclaim Salvation in Immanuel's name;
2. He'll shield you with a wall of fire, With holy zeal your hearts inspire,
3. And when our labors all are o'er, Then shall we meet to part no more;

To distant climes the tidings bear, And plant the rose of Sharon there.

Bid raging winds their fury cease, And calm the savage breast to peace.
Meet, with the blood-bought throng to fall, And crown the Saviour Lord of all.

The Gospel Feast.

1 Come, sinners, to the gospel feast,
Let every soul be Jesus' guest;
Ye need not one be left behind,
For God hath bidden all mankind.

2 Sent by my Lord, on you I call;
The invitation is to all:
Come, all the world! come, sinner thou!
All things in Christ are ready now.

3 My message as from God receive;
Ye all may come to Christ, and live;
O let his love your hearts constrain,
Nor suffer him to die in vain!

4 This is the time,— no more delay!
This is the Spirit's gracious day;
Come in this moment at his call,
And live for him who died for all.

All-sufficient grace.

1 Ho! every one that thirsts, draw nigh;
'Tis God invites the fallen race:
Mercy and free salvation buy,—
Buy wine, and milk, and gospel grace.

2 Come to the living waters, come!
Sinners, obey your Maker's call;
Return, ye weary wanderers, home,
And find his grace is free for all.

3 See from the Rock a fountain rise;
For you in healing streams it rolls;
Money ye need not bring, nor price,
Ye laboring, burdened, sin-sick souls.

4 Nothing ye in exchange shall give;
Leave all you have, and are, behind;
Frankly the gift of God receive;
Pardon and peace in Jesus find.

LENOX. H. M.

Edson.

1. Arise, my soul, arise, Shake off thy guilty fears; The bleeding sacrifice In my behalf appears; Before the throne my Surety stands, My name is written on his hands.

2 He ever lives above,
   For me to intercede
His all-redeeming love,
   His precious blood, to plead;
His blood atoned for all our race,
And sprinkles now the throne of grace.

3 Five bleeding wounds he bears,
   Received on Calvary;
They pour effectual prayers,
   They strongly plead for me:
Forgive him, O forgive, they cry,
Nor let that ransomed sinner die.

4 The Father hears him pray,
   His dear anointed One:
He cannot turn away
   The presence of his Son:
His Spirit answers to the blood,
And tells me I am born of God.

5 My God is reconciled;
   His pardoning voice I hear:
He owns me for his child;
   I can no longer fear:
With confidence I now draw nigh,
And Father, Abba Father, cry.

VICTORY. P. M. J. W. D.

Gentle and flowing style.

1. Happy the spir-it released from its clay; Happy the soul that goes bounding a-way; Singing as upward it hastes to the skies, "Victo-ry! victo-ry! homeward I rise. Many the toils it has passed through below, Many the

VICTORY, Concluded.

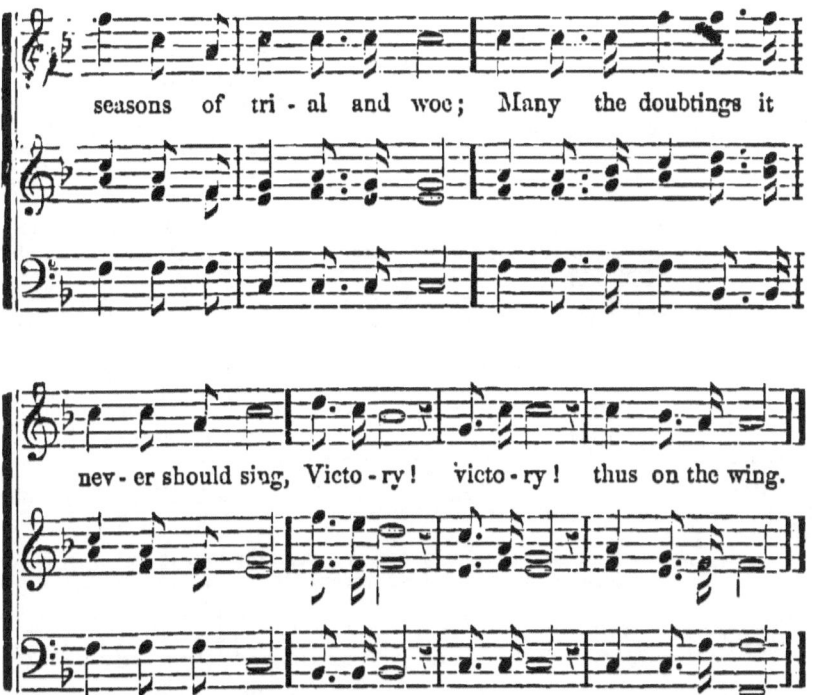

2 There lies the wearisome body at rest;
Closed are its eye-lids, and quiet its breast;
But the glad spirit, on pinions of light,
" Victory! victory!" sings in its flight.
While we are weeping our friends gone from earth,
Angels are singing their heavenly birth,
" Welcome, O welcome to our happy shore;
Victory! victory! weep ye no more."

3 How can we wish them recalled from their home,
Longer in sorrowing exile to roam?
Safely they passed from their troubles beneath,
" Victory! victory!" shouting in death.
Thus let them slumber, 'till Christ from the skies,
Bids them in glorified bodies arise;
Singing, as upward they spring from the tomb,
" Victory! victory! Jesus hath come."

REV. W. HUNTER.

CHINA. C. M.

T. Swan. 1800.

Vain man, thy fond pursuits forbear; Repent, thy end is nigh; Death, at the farthest, can't be far: O think before thou die.

Sin kills beyond the tomb.

2 Reflect, thou hast a soul to save;
Thy sins, how high they mount!
What are thy hopes beyond the grave?
How stands that dark account?

3 Death enters, and there's no defence;
His time there's none can tell;
He'll in a moment call thee hence,
To heaven, or down to hell.

4 Thy flesh (perhaps thy greatest care)
Shall into dust consume;
But, ah! destruction stops not there;
Sin kills beyond the tomb.

Why do we mourn.

1 Why do we mourn for dying friends,
Or shake at death's alarms?
'Tis but the voice that Jesus sends,
To call them to his arms.

2 Are we not tending upward too,
As fast as time can move?
Nor should we wish the hours more slow
To keep us from our love.

3 Why should we tremble to convey
Their bodies to the tomb?
There once the flesh of Jesus lay,
And left a long perfume.

4 The graves of all his saints he blest,
And softened every bed:
Where should the dying members rest,
But with their dying Head?

5 Thence he arose, ascending high,
And showed our feet the way;
Up to the Lord our flesh shall fly,
At the great rising day.

CAMBRIDGE. C. M.

Dr. Randall.

1. Daughter of Zi-on, from the dust Ex-alt thy fall-en head; A-gain in thy Re-deemer trust,— He calls thee from the dead, He calls thee from the dead, He calls thee from the dead.

Returning to Zion with songs of joy.

2 Awake, awake, put on thy strength,
Thy beautiful array;
The day of freedom dawns at length,—
The Lord's appointed day.

3 Rebuild thy walls, thy bounds enlarge,
And send thy heralds forth;
Say—to the south—Give up thy charge!
And— Keep not back, O north!

4 They come, they come: thine exiled bands,
Where'er they rest or roam,
Have heard thy voice in distant lands,
And hasten to their home.

5 Thus, though the universe shall burn,
And God his works destroy,
With songs thy ransomed shall return
And everlasting joy.

WELLS. L. M.

HOLDRAYD, 1753.

1. Life is the time to serve the Lord, The time t'insure the great reward;

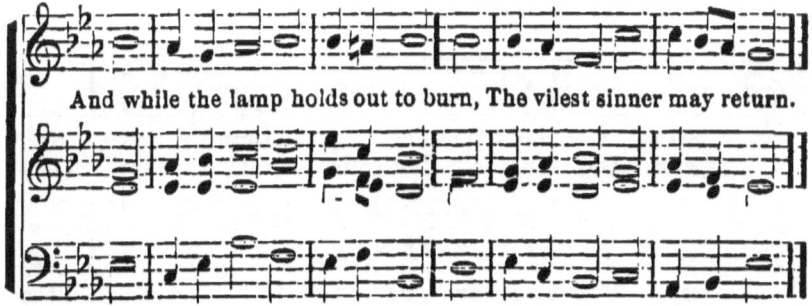

And while the lamp holds out to burn, The vilest sinner may return.

2 The living know that they must die:
But all the dead forgotten lie:
Their memory and their sense are gone,
Alike unknowing and unknown.

3 Life is the hour that God has given
T' escape from hell and fly to heaven;
The day of grace, and mortals may
Secure the blessings of the day.

4 Then what my thoughts design to do,
My hands, with all your might pursue,
Since no device, nor work is found,
Nor faith, nor hope beneath the ground.

Humble confession.

1 Saviour, I now with shame confess
My thirst for creature happiness;
By base desires I wrong'd thy love,
And forced thy mercy to remove.

2 Yet, O the riches of thy grace!
Thou, who hast seen my evil ways,
Wilt freely my backslidings heal,
And pardon on my conscience seal.

3 Yea, for thy truth and mercy's sake,
My comfort thou wilt give me back;
And lead me on from grace to grace,
In all the paths of righteousness:

4 Till fully saved my new-born soul,
And perfectly by faith made whole,
Shall bright in thy full image rise,
To share thy glory in the skies.

OLMUTZ. S. M. 131

Arranged by Dr. L. Mason.

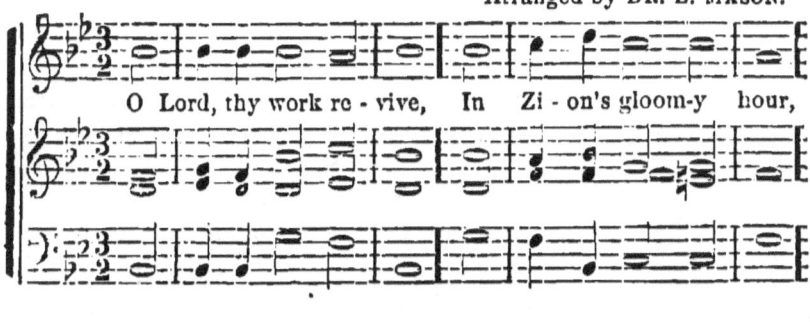

Dead in trespasses and sins.

1 O Lord, thy work revive,
  In Zion's gloomy hour,
And let our dying graces live,
  By thy restoring power.

2 O let thy chosen few
  Awake to earnest prayer;
Their covenant again renew,
  And walk in filial fear.

3 Thy Spirit then will speak
  Through lips of humble clay,
Till hearts of adamant shall break,—
  Till rebels shall obey.

4 Now lend thy gracious ear;
  Now listen to our cry;
O come, and bring salvation near;
  Our souls on thee rely.

1 How helpless nature lies,
  Unconscious of her load!
The heart unchanged can never rise
  To happiness and God.

2 Can aught but power divine
  The stubborn will subdue?
'Tis thine, eternal Spirit, thine
  To form the heart anew:—

3 The passions to recall,
  And upward bid them rise;
To make the scales of error fall
  From reason's darken'd eyes.

4 O change these hearts of ours,
  And give them life divine;
Then shall our passions and our powers,
  Almighty Lord, be thine.

CROSS AND CROWN. C. M.

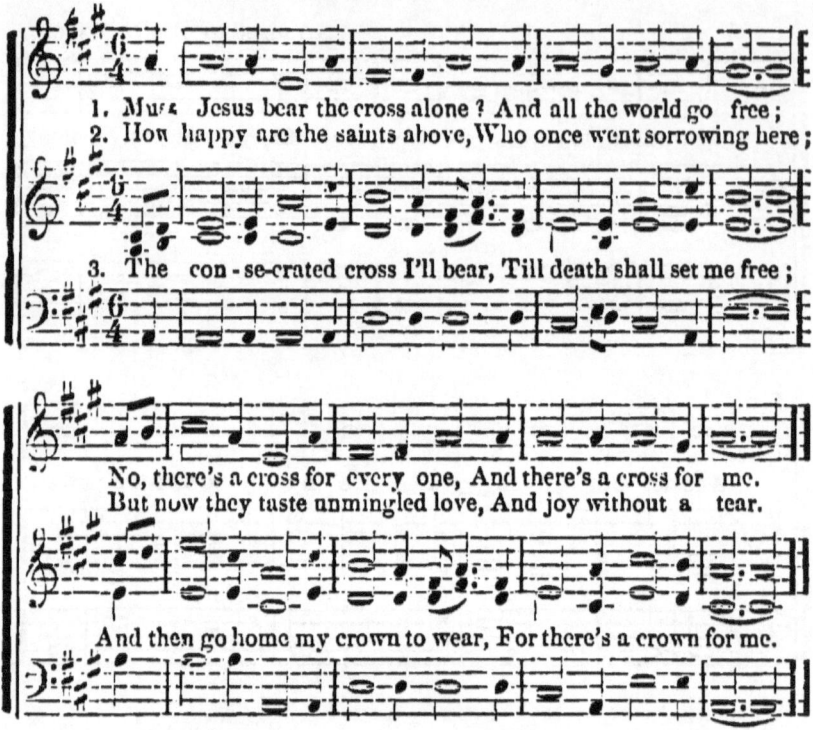

1. Must Jesus bear the cross alone? And all the world go free;
No, there's a cross for every one, And there's a cross for me.

2. How happy are the saints above, Who once went sorrowing here;
But now they taste unmingled love, And joy without a tear.

3. The con-se-crated cross I'll bear, Till death shall set me free;
And then go home my crown to wear, For there's a crown for me.

Remember me.

1 O Thou from whom all goodness flows,
   I lift my soul to thee;
In all my sorrows, conflicts, woes,
   O Lord, remember me.

2 If, for thy sake, upon my name
   Reproach and shame shall be,
I'll hail reproach, and welcome shame;
   O Lord, remember me.

3 When worn with pain, disease, and grief,
   This feeble body see;
Grant patience, rest, and kind relief;
   O Lord, remember me.

4 When, in the solemn hour of death,
   I wait thy just decree,
Be this the prayer of my last breath,—
   O Lord, remember me.

5 And when before thy throne I stand,
   And lift my soul to thee,
Then, with the saints at thy right hand,
   O Lord, remember me.

Goodness and mercy.

1 Let every tongue thy goodness speak,
   Thou sov'reign Lord of all;
Thy strength'ning hands uphold the weak
   And raise the poor that fall.

2 When sorrows bow the spirit down,
   When virtue lies distressed,
Beneath the proud oppressor's frown,
   Thou giv'st the mourner rest.

3 Thou know'st the pains thy servants feel,
   Thou hear'st thy children's cry;
And their best wishes to fulfil,
   Thy grace is ever nigh.

4 Thy mercy never shall remove
   From men of heart sincere;
Thou sav'st the souls whose humble love
   Is joined with holy fear.

5 My lips shall dwell upon thy praise,
   And spread thy fame abroad;
Let all the sons of Adam raise
   The honors of their God.

REST. L. M.   133

W. B. BRADBURY. By permission.

How blest the sacred tie that binds, In union sweet, according minds!

How swift the heavenly course they run, Whose hearts, and faith, and hopes are one.

"How blest the sacred tie."

2 To each the soul of each how dear!
What jealous care, what holy fear!
How doth the generous flame within,
Refine from earth and cleanse from sin!

3 Their streaming tears together flow
For human guilt and human woe;
Their ardent praise united rise,
Like mingling flames in sacrifice.

4 Together oft they seek the place
Where God reveals his awful face;
How high, how strong their raptures swell
There's none but kindred minds can tell.

5 Nor shall the glowing flame expire
'Mid nature's drooping, sickening fire:
Soon shall they meet in realms above,
A heaven of joy, because of love.

1 How vain is all beneath the skies!
How transient every earthly bliss!
How slender all the fondest ties
That bind us to a world like this!

2 The evening cloud, the morning dew,
The with'ring grass, the fading flower,
Of earthly hopes are emblems true,
The glory of a passing hour.

3 But though earth's fairest blossoms die,
And all beneath the skies is vain,
There is a brighter world on high,
Beyond the reach of care and pain.

4 Then let the hope of joys to come,
Dispel our cares, and chase our fears,
If God be ours, we're trav'ling home,
Though passing through a vale of tears

HOMEWARD BOUND. 10s & 4s. 135

Words by Rev. W. F. WARREN.   Arranged by J. W. D.

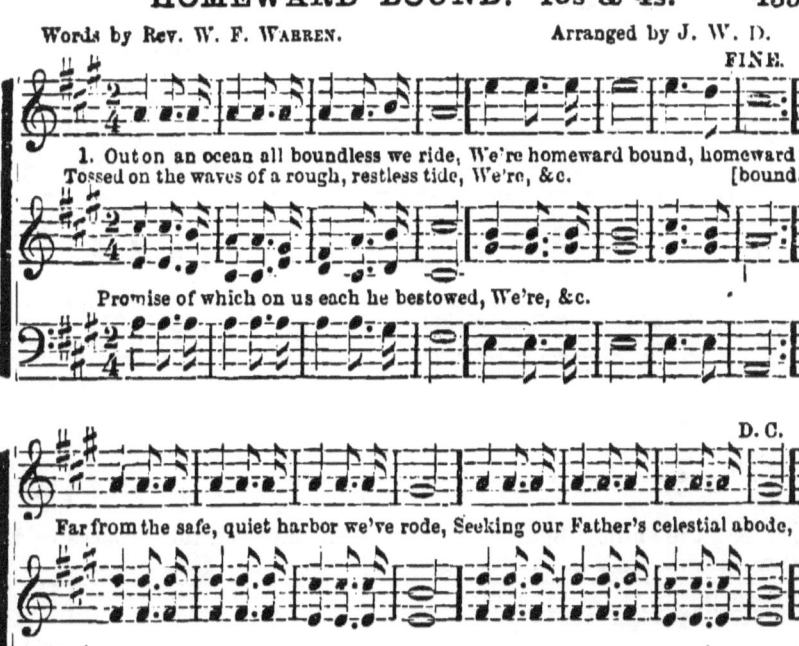

2 Wildly the storm sweeps us on as it roars,
  We're homeward bound.
Look! yonder lie the bright heavenly
    shores,
  We're homeward bound.
Steady, O pilot! stand firm at the wheel,
Steady, we soon shall outweather the gale,
O, how we fly 'neath the loud-creaking sail,
  We're homeward bound.

3 Down the horizon the earth disappears,
  We're homeward bound.
Joyful, O comrades! no sighing or tears,
  We're homeward bound.

Listen! what music comes soft o'er the sea,
  "Welcome, thrice welcome and blessed
    are ye."
Can it the greeting of Paradise be?
  We're homeward bound.

4 Into the harbor of heaven now we glide,
  We're home at last.
Softly we drift on its bright silver tide,
  We're home at last.
Glory to God! all our dangers are o'er,
We stand secure on the glorified shore;
Glory to God! we will shout evermore,
  We're home at last.

Conclusion of hymn on opposite page.

3 I've almost gained my heavenly home,
    My spirit loudly sings;
  The holy ones, behold, they come!
    I hear the noise of wings.

4 O, bear my longing heart to Him
    Who bled and died for me;
  Whose blood now cleanses from all sin,
    And gives me victory.

ELIZABETHTOWN. C. M.

Geo. Kingsley.

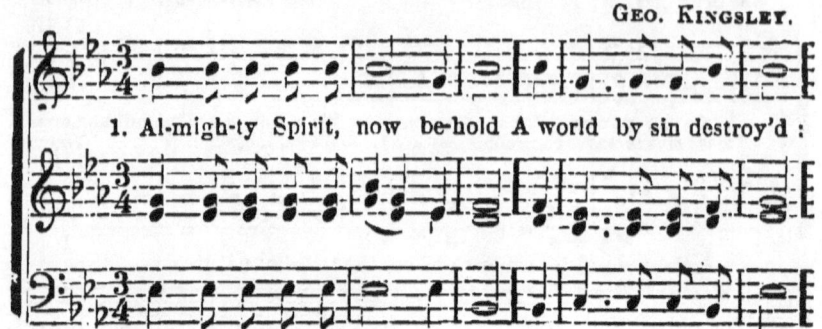

1. Al-migh-ty Spirit, now be-hold A world by sin destroy'd:

Cre-a-ting Spirit, as of old, Move on the formless void.

The earth renewed.

2 Give thou the word; that healing sound
Shall quell the deadly strife;
And earth again, like Eden crown'd,
Bring forth the tree of life.

3 If sang the morning stars for joy,
When nature rose to view,
What strains will angel-harps employ,
When thou shalt all renew!

4 And if the sons of God rejoice
To hear a Saviour's name,
How will the ransom'd raise their voice,
To whom the Saviour came!

5 Lo, every kindred, every tribe,
Assembling round the throne,
The new creation shall ascribe
To sov'reign love alone.

Spiritual influences.

1 Come, Holy Ghost, our hearts inspire;
Let us thine influence prove;—
Source of the old prophetic fire;
Fountain of life and love.

2 Come, Holy Ghost, for moved by thee
The prophets wrote and spoke:
Unlock the truth, thyself the key;
Unseal the sacred book.

3 Expand thy wings, Celestial Dove;
Brood o'er our nature's night;
On our disorder'd spirits move,
And let there now be light.

4 God, thro' himself, we then shall know
If thou within us shine;
And sound, with all thy saints below,
The depths of love divine.

HORTON. 6 lines. 7s. 137

GERMAN.

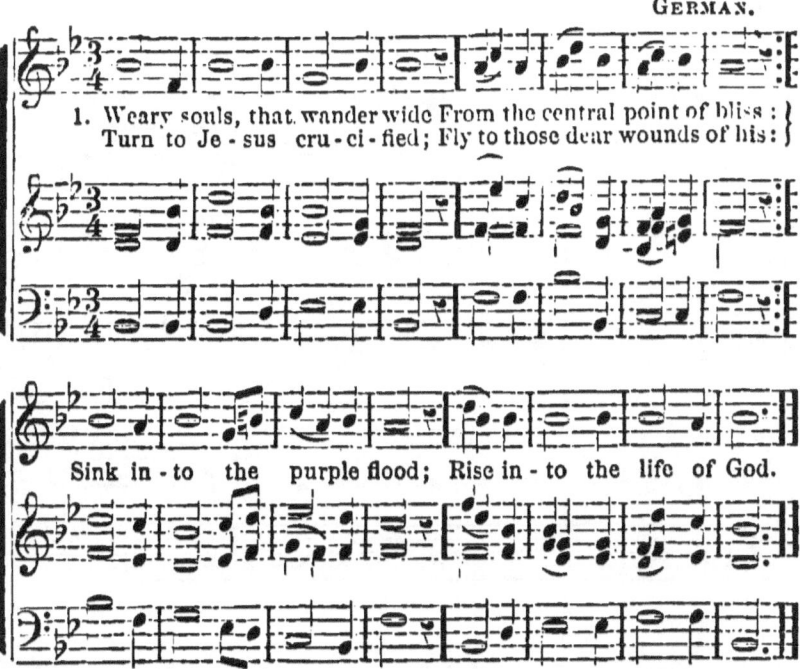

1. Weary souls, that wander wide From the central point of bliss:
Turn to Je-sus cru-ci-fied; Fly to those dear wounds of his:
Sink in-to the purple flood; Rise in-to the life of God.

Fly to Jesus.

2 Find in Christ the way of peace,
   Peace unspeakable, unknown;
By his pain he gives you ease,
   Life by his expiring groan:
Rise exalted by his fall;
Find in Christ your all in all.

3 O believe the record true,
   God to you his Son hath given;
Ye may now be happy too,
   Find on earth the life of heaven:
Live the life of heaven above,
All the life of glorious love.

4 This the universal bliss,
   Bliss for every soul design'd;
God's original promise this,
   God's great gift to all mankind:
Blest in Christ this moment be,
Blest to all eternity.

Clinging to the Cross.

1 Rock of ages, cleft for me,
   Let me hide myself in thee;
Let the water and the blood,
   From thy wounded side which flow'd,
Be of sin the double cure,—
Save from wrath, and make me pure.

2 Could my tears forever flow,—
   Could my zeal no languor know,—
These for sin could not atone;
   Thou must save, and thou alone:
In my hand no price I bring;
Simply to the cross I cling.

3 While I draw this fleeting breath,
   When my eyes shall close in death,
When I rise to worlds unknown,
   And behold thee on thy throne,—
Rock of ages, cleft for me,
Let me hide myself in thee

138. REST FOR THE WEARY. 8, 7, 5.

Revs. W. McD. and J W. D.

1. In the Christian's home in glory, There remains a land of rest;
There my Saviour's gone before me, To ful-fil my soul's request.

CHORUS.

There is rest for the weary, There is rest for the weary,
On the other side of Jordan, In the sweet fields of Eden,
There is rest for the weary, There is rest for you—
Where the tree of life is blooming, There is rest for you.

NETTLETON. 8s & 7s. Double. 139

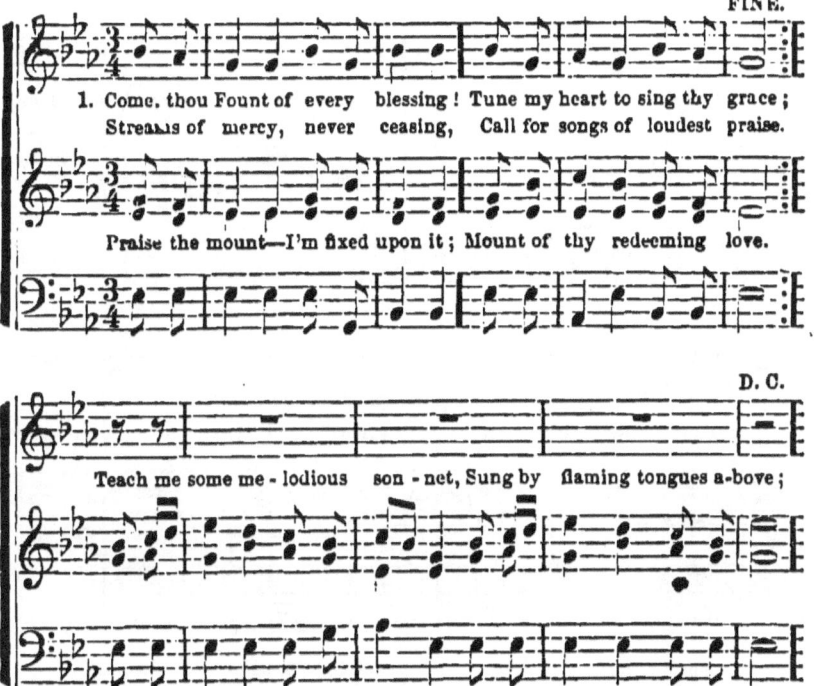

1. Come, thou Fount of every blessing! Tune my heart to sing thy grace;
Streams of mercy, never ceasing, Call for songs of loudest praise.
Praise the mount—I'm fixed upon it; Mount of thy redeeming love.
Teach me some me-lodious son-net, Sung by flaming tongues a-bove;

Hitherto hath the Lord helped us.

2 Here I'll raise mine Ebenezer;
Hither by thy help I'm come;
And I hope, by thy good pleasure,
Safely to arrive at home.
Jesus sought me when a stranger,
Wandering from the fold of God;
He, to rescue me from danger,
Interposed his precious blood.

3 O, to grace how great a debtor
Daily I'm constrained to be!
Let thy goodness, like a fetter,
Bind my wandering heart to thee:
Prone to wander, Lord, I feel it—
Prone to leave the God I love;
Here's my heart, O take and seal it;
Seal it for thy courts above.

Conclusion of hymn on opposite page.

2 He is fitting up my mansion,
Which eternally shall stand;
For my stay shall not be transient
In that holy, happy land.

3 Pain nor sickness ne'er shall enter,
Grief nor woe my lot shall share;
But in that celestial centre,
I a crown of life shall wear.

4 Death itself shall then be vanquished,
And his sting shall be withdrawn;
Shout for gladness, O ye ransomed!
Hail with joy the rising morn.

5 Sing, O sing, ye heirs of glory;
Shout your triumph as you go;
Zion's gates will open for you,
You shall find an entrance through.

ORTONVILLE. C. M.

Dr. Hastings.

1. Majestic sweetness sits enthroned Upon the Saviour's brow; His head with radiant glories crowned, His lips with grace o'erflow, His lips with grace o'erflow.

Indebtedness to Christ.

2 No mortal can with him compare
    Among the sons of men;
  Fairer is he than all the fair
    Who fill the heavenly train.

3 He saw me plunged in deep distress,
    And flew to my relief;
  For me he bore the shameful cross,
    And carried all my grief.

4 To him I owe my life and breath,
    And all the joys I have;
  He makes me triumph over death,
    And saves me from the grave.

5 Since from his bounty I receive
    Such proofs of love divine,
  Had I a thousand hearts to give,
    Lord, they should all be thine.

The Wanderer's Return.

1 O for a closer walk with God,—
    A calm and heavenly frame;
  A light to shine upon the road
    That leads me to the Lamb.

2 Where is the blessedness I knew
    When first I saw the Lord?
  Where is the soul-refreshing view
    Of Jesus and his word?

3 What peaceful hours I once enjoyed,
    How sweet their memory still!
  But they have left an aching void
    The world can never fill.

4 Return, O holy Dove, return,
    Sweet messenger of rest:
  I hate the sins that made thee mourn
    And drove thee from my breast.

5 The dearest idol I have known,
    Whate'er that idol be,
  Help me to tear it from thy throne,
    And worship only thee.

6 So shall my walk be close with God,
    Calm and serene my frame;
  So purer light shall mark the road
    That leads me to the Lamb.

HENDON. 7s.* 141

Rev. Dr. Malan.

Come, my soul, thy suit prepare; Jesus loves to answer prayer; He himself invites thee near, Bids thee ask him, waits to hear, Bids thee, &c.

1 Come, my soul, thy suit prepare;
Jesus loves to answer prayer;
He himself invites thee near,
Bids thee ask him, waits to hear.

2 Lord, I come to thee for rest;
Take possession of my breast;
There thy blood-bought right maintain,
And without a rival reign.

3 While I am a pilgrim here,
Let thy love my spirit cheer;
As my guide, my guard, my friend,
Lead me to my journey's end.

4 Show me what I have to do;
Every hour my strength renew;
Let me live a life of faith,—
Let me die thy people's death.

Life and immortality.

1 Day of God! thou blessed day,
At thy dawn the grave gave way
To the power of Him within,
Who had, sinless, bled for sin.

2 Thine the radiance to illume
First, for man, the dismal tomb,
When its bars their weakness own'd,
There revealing death dethroned.

3 Then the Sun of righteousness
Rose, a darken'd world to bless,
Bringing up from mortal night
Immortality and light.

4 Day of glory, day of power,
Sacred be thine every hour,—
Emblem, earnest, of the rest
That remaineth for the blest.

* Or 6 lines by repeating the first two.

NASHVILLE. L. P. M.

Arr. from a Gregorian Chant, by L. Mason, 1832. By permission.

1. Thou hidden Source of calm re-pose, Thou all-suf-ficient Love divine,
My help and refuge from my foes, Secure I am while thou art mine:
And lo! from sin, and grief, and shame,
I hide me, Jesus, in thy name.

Jesus all and in all.

2 Thy mighty name salvation is,
And keeps my happy soul above:
Comfort it brings, and power, and peace,
And joy, and everlasting love;
To me, with thy great name, are given
Pardon, and holiness, and heaven.

3 Jesus, my all in all thou art;
My rest in toil, my ease in pain;
The med'cine of my broken heart;
In war, my peace; in loss, my gain;
My smile beneath the tyrant's frown;
In shame, my glory and my crown.

4 In want, my plentiful supply;
In weakness, my almighty power;

In bonds, my perfect liberty;
My light, in Satan's darkest hour;
In grief, my joy unspeakable;
My life in death, my all in all.

Heal my backslidings.

1 O Jesus, full of truth and grace,—
More full of grace than I of sin,—
Yet once again I seek thy face;
Open thine arms and take me in!
And freely my backslidings heal,
And love the faithless sinner still.

2 Thou know'st the way to bring me back
My fallen spirit to restore;
O, for thy truth and mercy's sake,
Forgive, and bid me sin no more:
The ruins of my soul repair,
And make my heart a house of prayer.

3 Ah, give me, Lord, the tender heart,
That trembles at th' approach of sin
A godly fear of sin impart;
Implant and root it deep within,
That I may dread thy gracious power,
And never dare to' offend thee more

NORTHFIELD. C. M.

J. INGALLS.

1. O for a thousand tongues, to sing, My great Redeemer's praise; The glories of my God and King, The glories of my God and King, The triumphs of his grace.

General Invitation to praise the Redeemer.

2 My gracious Master, and my God,
   Assist me to proclaim,—
To spread, through all the earth abroad,
   The honors of thy Name.

3 Jesus! the Name that charms our fears,
   That bids our sorrows cease;
'Tis music in the sinner's ears,
   'Tis life, and health, and peace.

4 He breaks the power of cancelled sin,
   He sets the prisoner free;
His blood can make the foulest clean;
   His blood availed for me.

5 He speaks,—and, listening to his voice,
   New life the dead receive;
The mournful, broken hearts rejoice;
   The humble poor believe

I'M GOING HOME. L. M.

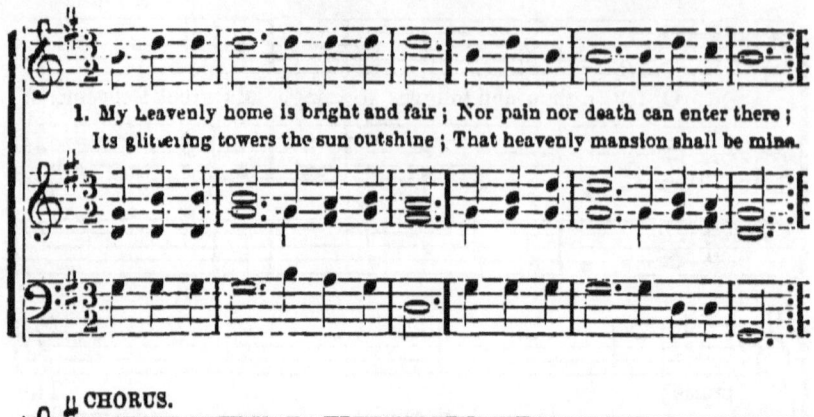

1. My heavenly home is bright and fair; Nor pain nor death can enter there;
Its glittering towers the sun outshine; That heavenly mansion shall be mine.

CHORUS.

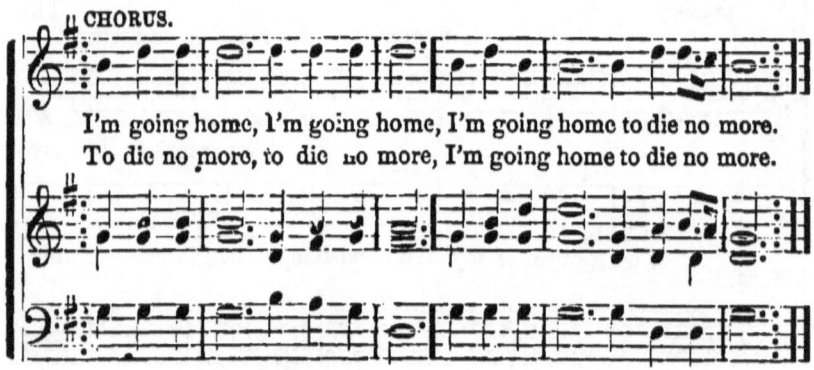

I'm going home, I'm going home, I'm going home to die no more.
To die no more, to die no more, I'm going home to die no more.

2 My Father's house is built on high,
Far, far above the starry sky;
When from this earthly prison free,
That heavenly mansion mine shall be.

3 While here, a stranger far from home,
Affliction's waves may round me foam;
And, though like Lazarus, sick and poor,
My heavenly mansion is secure.

4 Let others seek a home below,
Which flames devour, or waves o'erflow;
Be mine a happier lot to own
A heavenly mansion near the throne.

5 Then fail this earth, let stars decline,
And sun and moon refuse to shine,
All nature sink and cease to be,
That heavenly mansion stands for me.

REV W. HUNTER.

The Race for Glory.
TUNE, "NORTHFIELD."

1 Awake, my soul! stretch every nerve,
   And press with vigor on;
A heavenly race demands thy zeal,
   And an immortal crown.

2 'Tis God's all-animating voice
   That calls thee from on high;
'Tis he whose hand presents the prize
   To thine aspiring eye.

3 A cloud of witnesses around
   Hold thee in full survey;
Forget the steps already trod,
   And onward urge thy way.

4 Blest Saviour, introduced by thee,
   Our race have we begun;
And, crowned with victory, at thy feet
   We'll lay our trophies down.

LYONS. 10s & 11s. 145

The Lord will provide.

2 The birds, without barn or storehouse, are fed;
From them let us learn to trust for our bread:
His saints what is fitting shall ne'er be denied,
So long as 'tis written,—The Lord will provide.

3 When Satan appears to stop up our path,
And fills us with fear, we triumph by faith;
He cannot take from us (though oft he has tried)
The heart-cheering promise,—The Lord will provide.

4 He tells us we're weak,—our hope is in vain;
The good that we seek we ne'er shall obtain:
But when such suggestions our graces have tried,
This answers all questions,—The Lord will provide.

5 No strength of our own, nor goodness we claim:
Our trust is all thrown on Jesus's Name;
In this our strong tower for safety we hide;
The Lord is our power,—The Lord will provide.

6 When life sinks apace, and death is in view,
The word of his grace shall comfort us through;
Not fearing or doubting, with Christ on our side,
We hope to die shouting,—The Lord will provide.

146   MEAR. C. M.

ENGLISH TUNE.

1. O God, our help in a-ges past, Our hope for years to come, Our shelter from the stormy blast, And our e-ter-nal home.

God our help.

2 Under the shadow of thy throne
Still may we dwell secure;
Sufficient is thine arm alone,
And our defence is sure.

3 Before the hills in order stood,
Or earth received her frame,
From everlasting thou art God,
To endless years the same.

4 A thousand ages, in thy sight,
Are like an evening gone;
Short as the watch that ends the night,
Before the rising sun.

5 Time, like an ever rolling stream,
Bears all its sons away;
They fly, forgotten, as a dream
Dies at the opening day.

6 O God, our help in ages past,
Our hope for years to come;
Be thou our guide while life shall last,
And our perpetual home!

Vanity of earthly enjoyments.

1 How vain are all things here below;
How false, and yet how fair!
Each pleasure hath its poison too,
And every sweet a snare.

2 The brightest things below the sky
Give but a flattering light;
We should suspect some danger nigh,
Where we possess delight.

3 Our dearest joys, and nearest friends,
The partners of our blood,
How they divide our wavering minds,
And leave but half for God.

4 The fondness of a creature's love,
How strong it strikes the sense;
Thither the warm affections move,
Nor can we call them thence.

5 My Saviour, let thy beauties be
My soul's eternal food;
And grace command my heart away
From all created good.

HAMBURG. L. M.

L. MASON. By permission.

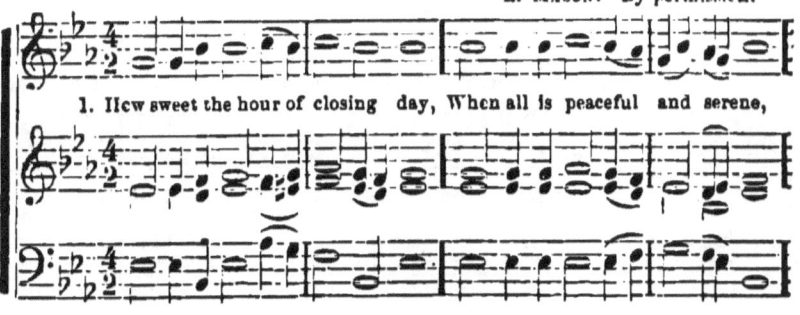

1. How sweet the hour of closing day, When all is peaceful and serene,

And when the sun, with cloudless ray, Sheds mellow lus-tre o'er the scene.

Christian's parting hour.

2 Such is the Christian's parting hour;
  So peacefully he sinks to rest;
  When faith, endued from heaven with power,
  Sustains and cheers his languid breast.

3 Mark but that radiance of his eye,
  That smile upon his wasted cheek;
  They tell us of his glory nigh,
  In language that no tongue can speak.

4 A beam from heaven is sent to cheer
  The pilgrim on his gloomy road;
  And angels are attending near,
  To bear him to their bright abode.

5 Who would not wish to die like those
  Whom God's own Spirit deigns to bless?
  To sink into that soft repose,
  Then wake to perfect happiness?

Memorials of His grace.

1 Thus far the Lord hath led me on,—
  Thus far his power prolongs my days;
  And every evening shall make known
  Some fresh memorial of his grace.

2 Much of my time has run to waste,
  And I, perhaps, am near my home;
  But he forgives my follies past,
  And gives me strength for days to come.

3 I lay my body down to sleep;
  Peace is the pillow for my head;
  While well-appointed angels keep
  Their watchful stations round my bed.

4 Thus, when the night of death shall [come,
  My flesh shall rest beneath the ground,
  And wait thy voice to rouse my tomb,
  With sweet salvation in the sound.

AMERICA. 6s & 4s.

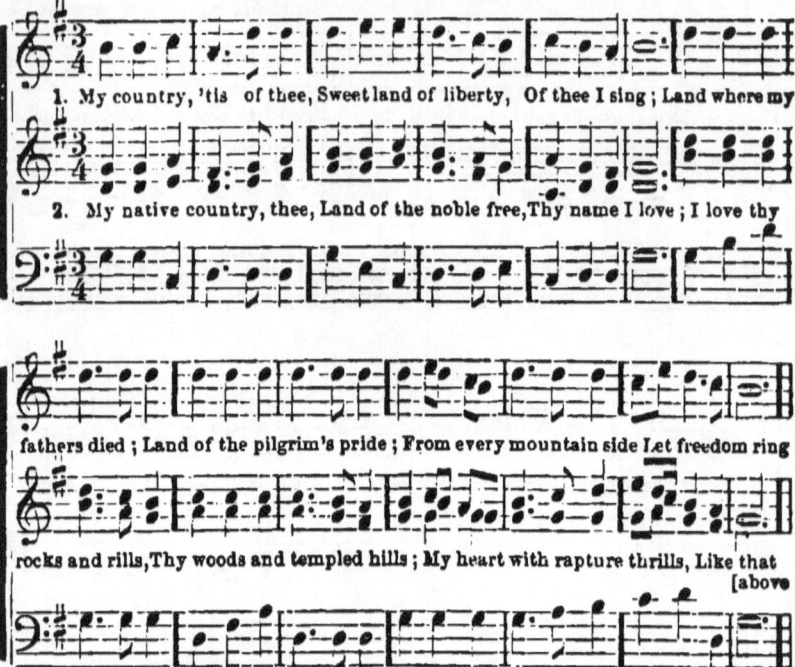

1. My country, 'tis of thee, Sweet land of liberty, Of thee I sing; Land where my fathers died; Land of the pilgrim's pride; From every mountain side Let freedom ring

2. My native country, thee, Land of the noble free, Thy name I love; I love thy rocks and rills, Thy woods and templed hills; My heart with rapture thrills, Like that [above

National Hymn.

3 Let music swell the breeze,
  And ring from all the trees
    Sweet freedom's song;
  Let mortal tongues awake;
  Let all that breathe partake;
  Let rocks their silence break—
    The sound prolong.

4 Our fathers' God, to thee,
  Author of liberty,
    To thee we sing:
  Long may our land be bright
  With freedom's holy light;
  Protect us by thy might,
    Great God, our King.

National Anniversary.

1 Auspicious morning, hail!
  Voices from hill and vale
    Thy welcome sing;
  Joy on thy dawning breaks;
  Each heart that joy partakes,
  While cheerful music wakes,
    Its praise to bring.

2 When on the tyrant's rod
  Our patriot fathers trod,
    And dared be free,
  'Twas not in burning zeal,
  Firm nerves, and hearts of steel,
  Our country's joy to seal,
    But, Lord, in thee.

3 Thou, as a shield of power,
  In battle's awful hour,
    Didst round us stand;
  Our hopes were in thy throne;
  Strong in thy might alone,
  By thee our banners shone,
    God of our land.

4 Long o'er our native hills,
  Long by our shaded rills,
    May freedom rest;
  Long may our shores have peace,
  Our flag grace every breeze;
  Our ships the distant seas,
    From east to west.

ITALIAN HYMN. 6s & 4s.   149
GIARDINI.

1. Come, thou Al-mighty King, Help us thy Name to sing, Help us to praise: Father all-glo-rious, O'er all vic-to-rious, Come, and reign o-ver us, Ancient of days.

Invocation of praise.

2 Jesus, our Lord, arise,
  Scatter our enemies,
    And make them fall;
  Let thine almighty aid
  Our sure defence be made;
  Our souls on thee be stayed;
    Lord, hear our call.

3 Come, thou incarnate Word,
  Gird on thy mighty sword,
    Our prayer attend;
  Come, and thy people bless,
  And give thy word success:
  Spirit of holiness,
    On us descend.

4 Come, holy Comforter,
  Thy sacred witness bear
    In this glad hour:
  Thou who Almighty art,
  Now rule in every heart,
  And ne'er from us depart,
    Spirit of power.

5 To the great One and Three
  Eternal praises be
    Hence, evermore.
  His sov'reign majesty
  May we in glory see,
  And to eternity
    Love and adore.

150 MERIBAH. C. P. M.

L. MASON. By permission.

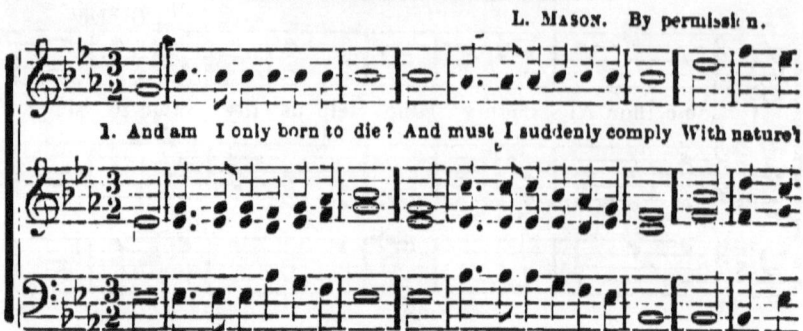

1. And am I only born to die? And must I suddenly comply With nature's

stern decree? { What after death for me remains? }
{ Ce-lestial joys or hellish pains, } To all e-ter-ni-ty.

The momentous question.

2 How then ought I on earth to live,
While God prolongs the kind reprieve,
   And props the house of clay?
My sole concern, my single care,
To watch, and tremble, and prepare
   Against that fatal day.

3 No room for mirth or trifling here,
For worldly hope, or worldly fear,
   If life so soon is gone;
If now the Judge is at the door,
And all mankind must stand before
   The' inexorable throne!

4 No matter which my thoughts employ,
A moment's misery or joy;
   But, O! when both shall end,
Where shall I find my destined place?
Shall I my everlasting days
   With fiends or angels spend?

5 Nothing is worth a thought beneath,
But how I may escape the death
   That never, never dies!
How make mine own election sure,
And when I fail on earth, secure
   A mansion in the skies.

6 Jesus, vouchsafe a pitying ray;
Be thou my Guide, be thou my Way
   To glorious happiness.
Ah! write the pardon on my heart;
And whensoe'er I hence depart,
   Let me depart in peace.

DEPTH OF MERCY. 7s.

Arranged by G. W. BALLOU. [By permission.]

2 I have long withstood his grace;
Long provoked him to his face;
Would not hearken to his calls;
Grieved him by a thousand falls.

3 Now incline me to repent;
Let me now my sins lament;
Now my foul revolt deplore,
Weep, believe, and sin no more.

4 Kindled his relentings are;
Me he now delights to spare;
Cries, How shall I give thee up?
Lets the lifted thunder drop.

5 There for me the Saviour stands;
Shows his wounds, and spreads his hands;
God is love! I know, I feel:
Jesus weeps, and loves me still

MASON. L. M. 153

1. My hope, my all, my Saviour thou, To thee, lo, now my soul I bow; I feel the bliss thy wounds impart, I find thee, Saviour, in my heart.

For sustaining grace.

2 Be thou my strength, be thou my way,
Protect me through my life's short day;
In all my acts may wisdom guide,
And keep me, Saviour, near thy side.

3 In fierce temptation's darkest hour,
Save me from sin and Satan's power;
Tear every idol from thy throne,
And reign, my Saviour, reign alone.

4 My suffering time shall soon be o'er;
Then shall I sigh and weep no more;
My ransomed soul shall soar away,
To sing thy praise in endless day.

Doxology.

Praise God, from whom all blessings flow;
Praise Him, all creatures here below;
Praise Him above, ye heavenly host;
Praise Father, Son, and Holy Ghost.

Conclusion of hymn on opposite page.

2 Come, sinners, see him lifted up,
　On the cross, on the cross.
He drinks for you the bitter cup,
　On the cross, on the cross.
To heaven he turns his languid eyes,
"'Tis finished," now the conqueror cries,
Then bows his sacred head and dies,
　On the cross, on the cross.

3 'Tis done! the mighty deed is done,
　On the cross, on the cross.
The battle fought, the victory won,
　On the cross, on the cross.
The rocks do rend, the mountains quake,
While Jesus doth atonement make,
While Jesus suffers for your sake,
　On the cross, on the cross.

4 Where'er I go I'll tell the story,
　Of the cross, of the cross.
In nothing else my soul shall glory,
　Save the cross, save the cross.
Yes, this my constant theme shall be,
Through time, and in eternity,
That Jesus suffered death for me,
　On the cross, on the cross.

5 Let every mourner come and cling
　To the cross, to the cross.
Let every Christian come and sing,
　Round the cross, round the cross.
Here let the preacher take his stand,
And with the Bible in his hand,
Proclaim the triumphs of the Lamb,
　On the cross, on the cross.

MENDON. L. M.

GERMAN AIR.

Servants of God! in joy-ful lays, Sing ye the Lord Jehovah's praise;

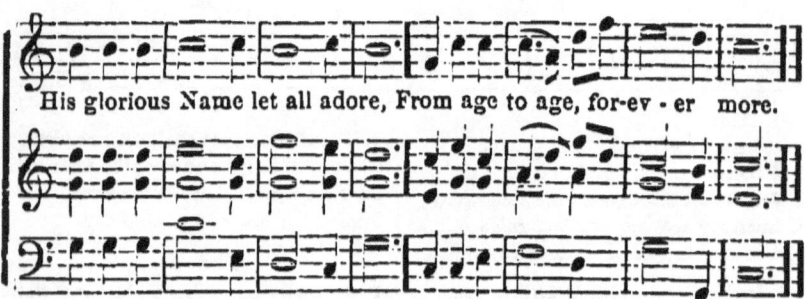

His glorious Name let all adore, From age to age, for-ev-er more.

217 *The glories of Jehovah.*

2 Blest be that Name, supremely blest,
From the sun's rising to its rest;
Above the heavens his power is known,
Thro' all the earth his goodness shown.

3 Who is like God? so great, so high,
He bows himself to view the sky;
And yet, with condescending grace,
Looks down upon the human race.

4 He hears the uncomplaining moan
Of those who sit and weep alone.
He lifts the mourner from the dust;
In Him the poor may safely trust.

5 O then, aloud, in joyful lays,
Sing to the Lord Jehovah's praise;
His saving Name let all adore,
From age to age, forever more.

218 *The bond of love.*

1 Praise waits in Zion, Lord, for thee;
Thy saints adore thy holy name;
Thy creatures bend th' obedient knee,
And, humbly, now thy presence claim.

2 Eternal Source of truth and light,
To thee we look, on thee we call;
Lord, we are nothing in thy sight,
But thou to us art all in all.

3 Still may thy children in thy word
Their common trust and refuge see;
O, bind us to each other, Lord,
By one great bond,—the love of thee.

4 So shall our sun of hope arise,
With brighter still and brighter ray,
Till thou shalt bless our longing eyes
With beams of everlasting day.

ARLINGTON. C. M.

DR. ARNE.

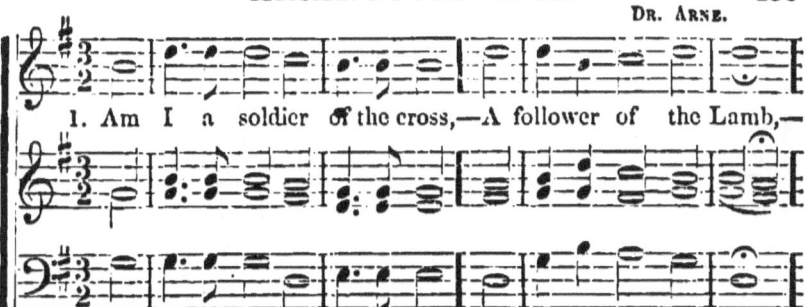

1. Am I a soldier of the cross,—A follower of the Lamb,—

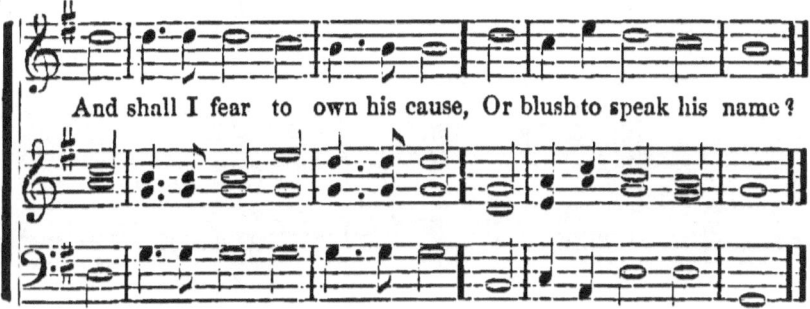

And shall I fear to own his cause, Or blush to speak his name?

Faith sees the final triumph.

2 Must I be carried to the skies
　On flowery beds of ease;
While others fought to win the prize,
　And sailed through bloody seas?

3 Are there no foes for me to face?
　Must I not stem the flood?
Is this vile world a friend to grace,
　To help me on to God?

4 Since I must fight if I would reign,
　Increase my courage, Lord;
I'll bear the toil, endure the pain,
　Supported by thy word.

5 Thy saints in all this glorious war
　Shall conquer, though they die;
They see the triumph from afar,—
　By faith they bring it nigh.

6 When that illustrious day shall rise,
　And all thy armies shine
In robes of victory through the skies,
　The glory shal be thine.

Walk in the Light.

1 Walk in the light! so shalt thou know
　That fellowship of love,
His Spirit only can bestow
　Who reigns in light above.

2 Walk in the light! and thou shalt find
　Thy heart made truly his
Who dwells in cloudless light enshrined,
　In whom no darkness is.

3 Walk in the light! and thou shalt own
　Thy darkness passed away,
Because that Light hath on thee shone
　In which is perfect day.

4 Walk in the light! and e'en the tomb
　No fearful shade shall wear;
Glory shall chase away its gloom,
　For Christ hath conquered there.

5 Walk in the light! thy path shall be
　Peaceful, serene, and bright:
For God, by grace, shall dwell in thee,
　And God himself is light.

CONCORD. S. M. 157
O. HOLDEN. 1793.

Glory begun below.

1 Come, ye that love the Lord,
   And let your joys be known;
   Join in a song with sweet accord,
   While ye surround his throne.
   Let those refuse to sing
   Who never knew our God,
   But servants of the heavenly King
   May speak their joys abroad.

2 The men of grace have found
   Glory begun below;
   Celestial fruit on earthly ground
   From faith and hope may grow:
   Then let our songs abound,
   And every tear be dry:
   We're marching thro' Immanuel's ground,
   To fairer worlds on high.

Conclusion of hymn on opposite page.

2 There is a place where the angels dwell,
   A pure and a peaceful abode;
The joys of that place no tongue can tell,
   But there is the palace of God.

3 There is a place where my friends are gone,
   Who suffered and worshipped with me;

Exalted with Christ high on his throne,
   The King in his beauty they see.

4 There is a place where I hope to live,
   When life and its labors are o'er;
A place which the Lord to me will give,
   And then I shall sorrow no more.

REV W. HUNTER.

I'M A TRAVELLER.

N. BILLINGS.

1. I'm a lonely trav'ler here, Weary, oppressed; But my journey's end is near; Soon I shall rest. Dark and dreary is the way, Toiling I've come; Ask me not with you to stay, Yonder's my home.

2 I'm a weary traveller here,
  I must go on;
For my journey's end is near;
  I must be gone:
Brighter joys than earth can give
  Win me away;
Pleasures that forever live;
  I cannot stay.

3 I'm a traveller to a land
  Where all is fair;
Where are seen no broken bands;
  All, all are there;
Where no tears shall ever fall,
  No heart be sad;.
Where the glory is for all,
  And all are glad.

4 I'm a traveller, and I go
  Where all is fair;
Farewell all I've loved below;
  I must be there.
Worldly honors, hopes and gain,
  All I resign;
Welcome sorrow, grief, and pain
  If heaven be mine.

5 I'm a traveller; call me not;
  Upward's my way;
Yonder is my rest and lot;
  I cannot stay.
Farewell, earthly pleasures all;
  Pilgrim I'll roam;
Hail me not; in vain you call;
  Yonder's my home.

JUST AS I AM. 8s & 6s.

J. W. D.

1. Just as I am, with-out one plea, But that thy blood was shed for me, And that thou bid'st me come to thee, O Lamb of God, I come, I come; O Lamb of God, I come.

2. Just as I am, and wait-ing not, To rid my soul of one dark blot; To thee, whose blood can cleanse each spot, O Lamb of God, I come, I come; O Lamb of God, I come.

3 Just as I am—poor, wretched, blind;
Sight, riches, healing of the mind,
Yea, all I need, in thee I find,
   O Lamb of God, I come.

4 Just as I am—though tossed about,
With many a conflict, many a doubt;
Fightings within, and fears without—
   O Lamb of God, I come.

5 Just as I am—thou wilt receive,
Wilt welcome, pardon, cleanse, relieve,
Because thy promise I believe—
   O Lamb of God, I come.

6 Just as I am—thy love unknown
Has broken every barrier down;
Now to be thine, yea, thine alone,
   O Lamb of God, I come

BETHLEHEM. 8s & 7s.

1. Glorious things of thee are spoken, Zion, ci-ty of our God;
He, whose word cannot be broken, Form'd thee for his own abode;
With salvation's walls surrounded, Thou may'st smile at all thy foes.
On the Rock of ages founded, What can shake thy sure repose?

2 See, the streams of living waters,
   Springing from eternal love,
Still supply thy sons and daughters,
   And all fear of want remove:
Who can faint while such a river
   Ever flows our thirst to' assuage?
Grace, which, like the Lord, the giver,
   Never fails from age to age.

3 Round each habitation hovering,
   See the cloud and fire appear!
For a glory and a covering,
   Showing that the Lord is near:
He who gives us daily manna,
   He who listens when we cry,
Let him hear the loud Hosanna
   Rising to his throne on high.

SILVER STREET. S. M.

I. Smith.

1. Come, sound his praise abroad, And hymns of glo-ry sing: Jehovah is the sov'-reign God, The u - - ni - ver-sal King.

2 Come, worship at his throne;
Come, bow before the Lord;
We are his work, and not our own,
He formed us by his word.

3 To-day attend his voice,
Nor dare provoke his rod;
Come, like the people of his choice,
And own your gracious God.

Hymns for tune on opposite page.

Spirit's quickening influences.

1 Come, thou everlasting Spirit,
  Bring to every thankful mind
All the Saviour's dying merit,
  All his sufferings for mankind:
True recorder of his passion,
  Now the living faith impart;
Now reveal his great salvation
  Unto every faithful heart.

2 Come, thou Witness of his dying;
  Come, Remembrancer divine;
Let us feel thy power applying
  Christ to every soul and mine;
Let us groan thine inward groaning;
  Look on Him we pierced, and grieve;
All partake the grace atoning,—
  All the sprinkled blood receive.

The heavenly banquet.

1 Jesus spreads his banner o'er us,
  Cheers our famished souls with food;
He the banquet spreads before us,
  Of his mystic flesh and blood.
Precious banquet; bread of heaven;
  Wine of gladness, flowing free;
May we taste it, kindly given,
  In remembrance, Lord, of thee.

2 In thy holy incarnation,
  When the angels sang thy birth
In thy fasting and temptation;
  In thy labors on the earth;
In thy trial and rejection;
In thy sufferings on the tree;
In thy glorious resurrection;
  May we, Lord, remember thee.

GLORY TO THE LAMB. 163

REV. W. B. GORMAN.

1. The world is ov-er-come by the blood of the Lamb!
   The world is ov-er-come by the blood of the Lamb!
2. My sins are washed a-way in the blood of the Lamb!

Glory to the Lamb! Glory to the Lamb! Glory to the Lamb!

3 The devil's overcome by the blood of the Lamb! Glory, &c.

4 I've lost the fear of death through the blood of the Lamb! Glory &c.

5 The martyrs overcame by the blood of the Lamb! Glory, &c.

6 I hope to gain the skies by the blood of the Lamb! Glory, &c.

Conclusion of hymn on opposite page.

2 Fear ye not the way so lonely,
 You, a feeble band?
No, for friends unseen are near us,
 Angels round us stand;
Christ, our leader, walks beside us,
He will guard, and He will guide us,
He will guard, and He will guide us,
 To the better land.

3 Tell me, pilgrims, what you hope for,
 In the better land?
Spotless robes and crowns of glory,
 From a Saviour's hand;

We shall drink of life's clear river,
We shall dwell with God forever,
We shall dwell with God forever,
 In the better land

4 Will you let me travel with you
 To the better land?
Come away, we bid you welcome
 To our little band.
Come, O come! we cannot leave you,
Christ is waiting to receive you,
Christ is waiting to receive you,
 In the better land.

SWEET REST IN HEAVEN.

W. B. BRADBURY. By permission.

Sweet rest in Jesus.

2 Loved ones have gone before us,
  They beckon us away;
O'er aerial plains they're soaring,
  Blest in eternal day;
But we are in the army,
  And dare not leave our post;
We'll fight until we conquer
  The foe's most mighty host.
    There is sweet rest, &c.

3 Our Captain's gone before us,
  He kindly calls us home
To yonder worlds of glory,
  And sweetly bids us come.
The world, the flesh, and Satan,
  Will strive to hedge our way;
But we'll overcome these powers,—
  We'll hourly watch and pray.
    There is sweet rest, &c.

I LOVE THEE. P. M.

165

Arranged by J. W. D.

1. I love thee, I love thee, I love thee, my Lord; I love thee, my Saviour; I love thee, my God; I love thee, I love thee, and long to be there, With Jesus and angels, my kindred so dear.

2. I'm happy, I'm happy, O, wondrous account! My joys are immortal, I stand on the mount! I gaze on my treasure, and that thou dost know; But how much I love thee, I never can show.

3 O Jesus, my Saviour, with thee I am blest!
My life and salvation, my joy and my rest!
Thy name be my theme, and thy love be my song,
Thy grace shall inspire both my heart and my tongue.

4 O, who's like my Saviour? He's Salem's bright King;
He smiles, and he loves me, and learns me to sing;
I'll praise him, I'll praise him, with notes loud and shrill,
While rivers of pleasure my spirit doth fill.

THE EDEN ABOVE. 12s & 11s.

Arr. by J. W. D.

1. We're bound for the land of the pure and the ho-ly, The home of the happy, the kingdom of love;
Ye wanderers from God in the broad road of fol-ly, O say, will you go to the Eden above?

CHORUS. Will you go, will you go, will you go, will you go? O say, will you go to the Eden above?

2.
In that blessed land neither sighing nor anguish
Can breathe in the fields where the glorified rove;
Ye heart-burdened ones, who in misery languish,
O say, will you go to the Eden above?
CHORUS.

3.
No poverty there—no, the saints are all wealthy,
The heirs of his glory whose nature is love;
Nor sickness can reach them, that country is healthy;
O say, will you go to the Eden above?
CHORUS.

EXPOSTULATION. 11s.

1. O turn ye, O turn ye, for why will you die,
When God in great mercy is coming so nigh?
D. C. And angels are waiting to welcome you home.
Since Jesus invites you, the Spirit says, Come,

2 How vain the delusion, that while you delay,
Your hearts may grow better by staying away;
Come wretched, come starving, come just as you be,
While streams of salvation are flowing so free.

3 And now Christ is ready your souls to receive,
O, how can you question, if you will believe?
If sin is your burden, why will you not come?
'Tis you he bids welcome; he bids you come home.

4 In riches, in pleasures, what can you obtain,
To soothe your affliction, or banish your pain;
To bear up your spirit when summoned to die,
Or waft you to mansions of glory on high?

5 Come, give us your hand, and the Saviour your heart,
And trusting in Heaven, we never shall part;
O how can we leave you? why will you not come?
We'll journey together, and soon be at home.

Conclusion of hymn on opposite page.

4.
March on, happy pilgrims, that land is before you,
And soon its ten thousand delights we shall prove;
Yes, soon we shall walk o'er the hills of bright glory,
And drink the pure joys of the Eden above.
We will go, &c.
O yes, we will go to the Eden above.

5.
And yet, guilty sinner, we would not forsake thee,
We halt yet a moment as onward we move;
O come to thy Lord, in his arms he will take thee,
And bear thee along to the Eden above.
Will you go, &c.
O say, will you go to the Eden above?

6.
Methinks thou art now in thy wretchedness saying,
O, who can this guilt from my conscience remove?
No other but Jesus; then come to him praying—
Prepare me, O Lord, for the Eden above.
Will you go, &c.
At last, will you go to the Eden above?

REV. W. HUNTER

170. EXHORTATION. C. M.

HIBBARD.

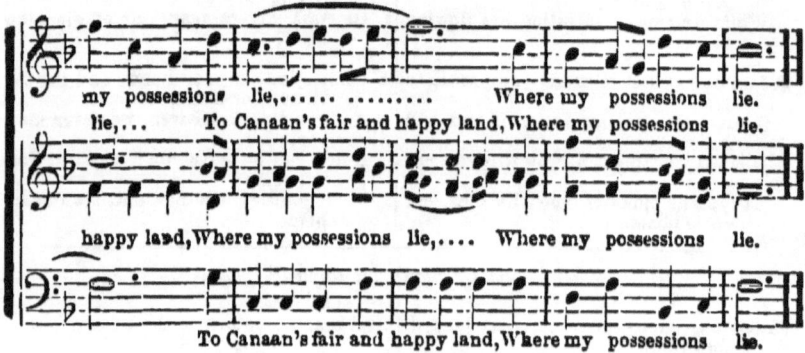

The promised land.

2 O the transporting, rapturous scene,
  That rises to my sight!
Sweet fields arrayed in living green,
  And rivers of delight.

3 There generous fruits that never fail,
  On trees immortal grow;
There rock, and hill, and brook, and vale,
  With milk and honey flow.

4 O'er all those wide extended plains
  Shines one eternal day;
There God the Son forever reigns,
  And scatters night away.

5 No chilling winds, or poisonous breath,
  Can reach that healthful shore;
Sickness and sorrow, pain and death,
  Are felt and feared no more.

BALERMA. C. M.

R. SIMPSON.

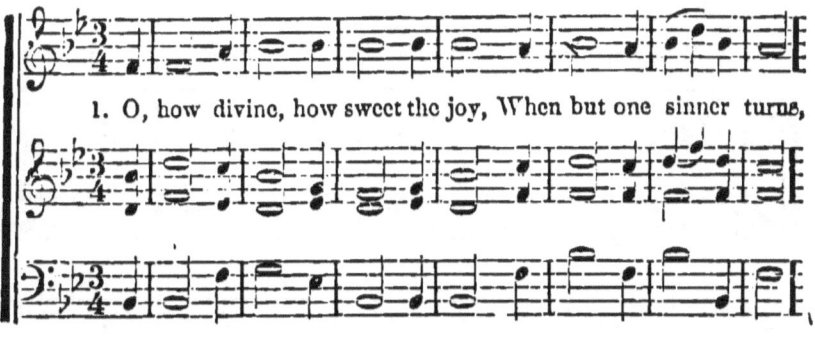

1. O, how divine, how sweet the joy, When but one sinner turns,

And with an humble, broken heart, His sin and er-ror mourns!

Joy over the repenting sinner.

1 O, how divine, how sweet the joy,
   When but one sinner turns,
And with an humble, broken heart,
   His sin and error mourns!

2 Pleased with the news, the saints below
   In songs their tongues employ;
Beyond the skies the tidings go,
   And heaven is filled with joy.

3 Well pleased, the Father sees and hears
   The conscious sinner's moan;
Jesus receives him in his arms,
   And claims him for his own.

4 Nor angels can their joys contain,
   But kindle with new fire:
"The sinner lost is found," they sing,
   And strike the sounding lyre.

The pledge of joys to come.

1 Why should the children of a King
   Go mourning all their days?
Great Comforter, descend and bring
   The tokens of thy grace.

2 Dost thou not dwell in all thy saints,
   And seal the heirs of heaven?
When wilt thou banish my complaints,
   And show my sins forgiven?

3 Assure my conscience of her part
   In the Redeemer's blood;
And bear thy witness with my heart,
   That I am born of God.

4 Thou art the earnest of his love,
   The pledge of joys to come;
May thy blest wings, celestial Dove,
   Safely convey me home.

WATCHMAN, TELL US OF THE NIGHT.

The Watchman's report.

2 Watchman, tell us of the night;
　Higher yet that star ascends.
Trav'ler, blessedness and light,
　Peace and truth, its course portends.
Watchman, will its beams, alone,
　Gild the spot that gave them birth?
Trav'ler, ages are its own;
　See, it bursts o'er all the earth.

3 Watchman, tell us of the night,
　For the morning seems to dawn.
Trav'ler, darkness takes its flight;
　Doubt and terror are withdrawn.
Watchman, let thy wandering cease;
　Hie thee to thy quiet home.
Trav'ler, lo! the Prince of Peace,
　Lo! the Son of God is come.

The only Refuge.

1 Jesus, lover of my soul,
　Let me to thy bosom fly,
While the nearer waters roll,
　While the tempest still is high;
Hide me, O my Saviour, hide,
　Till the storm of life is past;
Safe into the haven guide,
　O receive my soul at last.

2 Other refuge have I none;
　Hangs my helpless soul on thee:
Leave, O leave me not alone;
　Still support and comfort me:
All my trust on thee is stayed;
　All my help from thee I bring;
Cover my defenceless head
　With the shadow of thy wing.

3 Thou, O Christ, art all I want:
　More than all in thee I find:
Raise the fallen, cheer the faint,
　Heal the sick, and lead the blind.
Just and holy is thy name;
　I am all unrighteousness;
False, and full of sin I am;
　Thou art full of truth and grace.

4 Plenteous grace with thee is found,—
　Grace to cover all my sin:
Let the healing streams abound,
　Make and keep me pure within.
Thou of life the fountain art;
　Freely let me take of thee:
Spring thou up within my heart;
　Rise to all eternity.

The cry of the heathen.
TUNE, "MISSIONARY HYMN."

1 From Greenland's icy mountains,
　From India's coral strand;
Where Afric's sunny fountains
　Roll down their golden sand;
From many an ancient river,
　From many a palmy plain,
They call us to deliver
　Their land from error's chain.

2 What though the spicy breezes
　Blow soft o'er Ceylon's isle;
Though every prospect pleases,
　And only man is vile:
In vain with lavish kindness
　The gifts of God are strown;
The heathen in his blindness
　Bows down to wood and stone.

3 Shall we, whose souls are lighted
　With wisdom from on high,
Shall we to men benighted
　The lamp of life deny?
Salvation! O salvation!
　The joyful sound proclaim,
Till earth's remotest nation
　Has learned Messiah's name.

4 Waft, waft, ye winds, his story,
　And you, ye waters, roll,
Till, like a sea of glory,
　It spreads from pole to pole:
Till o'er our ransomed nature
　The Lamb for sinners slain,
Redeemer, King, Creator,
　In bliss returns to reign.

NO NIGHT IN HEAVEN.

J. W. D

"And there shall be no night there."—Rev. xxii. 5.

1. No night shall be in heaven! No gath'ring gloom Shall o'er that glorious landscape ev-er come: No tears shall fall in sadness o'er those flowers, That breathe their fragrance thro' celestial bowers.

2 No night shall be in Heaven! no dreadful hour
Of mental darkness, or the tempter's power;
Across those skies no envious cloud shall roll,
To dim the sunlight of the raptured soul.

3 No night shall be in Heaven! no sorrow's reign,
No secret anguish, no corporeal pain;
No shivering limbs, no burning fever there:
No soul's eclipse, no winter of despair.

PLEADING SAVIOUR. 8s & 7s. 175

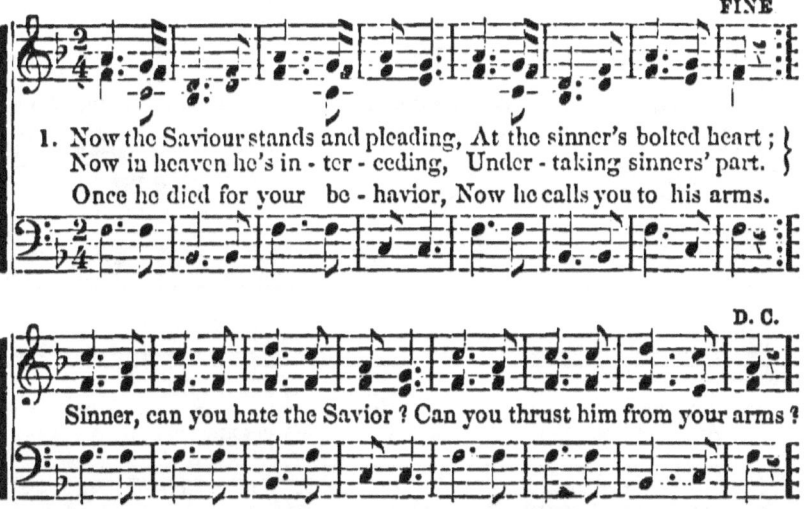

1. Now the Saviour stands and pleading, At the sinner's bolted heart;
Now in heaven he's in-ter-ceding, Under-taking sinners' part.
Once he died for your be-havior, Now he calls you to his arms.
Sinner, can you hate the Savior? Can you thrust him from your arms?

2 Jesus stands, O how amazing,
Stands and knocks at every door;
In his hands ten thousand blessings,
Proffered to the wretched poor.

3 See him bleeding, dying, rising,
To prepare you heavenly rest;
Listen, while he kindly calls you,
Hear, and be forever blest.

4 Now he has not come to judgment,
To condemn your wretched race;
But to ransom ruined sinners,
And display unbounded grace.

5 Will you plunge in endless darkness,
There to bear eternal pain;
Or to realms of glorious brightness
Rise, and with him ever reign?

Conclusion of hymn on opposite page.

4 No night shall be in Heaven—but endless noon;
No fast-declining sun, nor waning moon;
But there the LAMB shall yield perpetual light,
'Mid pastures green, and waters ever bright.

5 No night shall be in Heaven—no darkened room,
No bed of death, nor silence of the tomb;
But breezes, ever fresh with love and truth,
Shall brace the frame with an immortal youth.

6 No night shall be in Heaven! but night is here,
The night of sorrow, and the night of fear;
I mourn the ills that now my steps attend,
And shrink from others that may yet impend.

7 No night shall be in Heaven! O, had I faith
To rest in what the faithful Witness saith,
That faith should make these hideous phantoms flee,
And leave no night, henceforth, on earth, to me.

TO MY MOTHER IN HEAVEN. C. M.

1. The night comes stealing on, mother, With gentle, loving tone, And here be-side thy grave I stand, Sweet mother, all a-lone. Ah! many an eve has passed a-way, Bright suns have rose and set, Fair moons have come and gone again, Since last, since last we met.

ST. THOMAS. S. M.

HANDEL.

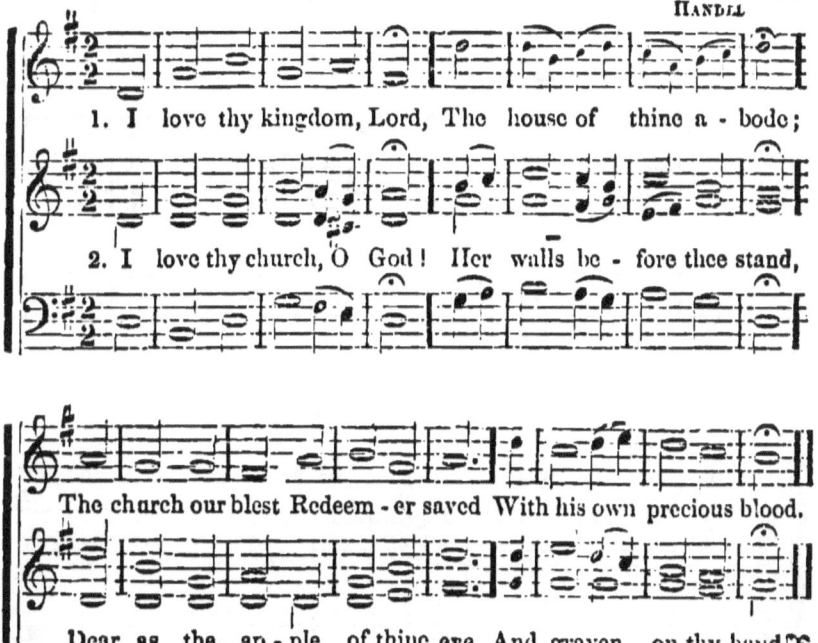

1. I love thy kingdom, Lord, The house of thine a-bode;
2. I love thy church, O God! Her walls be-fore thee stand,

The church our blest Redeem-er saved With his own precious blood.
Dear as the ap-ple of thine eye, And graven on thy hand.

3 For her my tears shall fall:
For her my prayers ascend
To her my cares and toils be given,
Till toils and cares shall end.

4 Beyond my highest joy
I prize her heavenly ways,
Her sweet communion, solemn vows,
Her hymns of love and praise.

Conclusion of hymn on opposite page.

2 My heart is sad to-night, mother,
E'en sadder than before;
For memory wanders far, far back
To happy scenes of yore.
To golden, halcyon, dreaming days,
When often at thy feet,
I sat me down to weave fair flowers,
In garlands fresh and sweet.

3 And then around my brow, mother,
Those garlands you would twine,
And murmur, may life's fairest flowers,
My darling, e'er be thine.

Then let me, let me weep to night
O'er life's now withered flowers,
Whose fragrance filled my youthful breast
In earlier, happier hours.

4 I'm kneeling by thy grave, mother,
To wait thy blessing given,
And list the whispered words of love
Borne from thy home in Heaven.
And now I leave thy resting-place,
To come again no more,
Till autumn's plaintive moan is heard
From summer's leafy shore

LETA LYNDON.

178 A HOME IN HEAVEN. P. M.

1. A home in heaven! what a joyful thought, As the poor man toils in his weary lot! His heart oppressed, and with anguish driven, From his home below, to his home in heaven.

2 A home in heaven! as the sufferer lies
On his bed of pain, and uplifts his eyes
To that bright home; what a joy is given,
With the blessed thought of his home in heaven.

3 A home in heaven! when our pleasures fade,
And our wealth and fame in the dust are laid;
And strength decays, and our health is riven,
We are happy still with our home in heaven.

WATCHMAN. S. M. 179
JAMES LEACH.

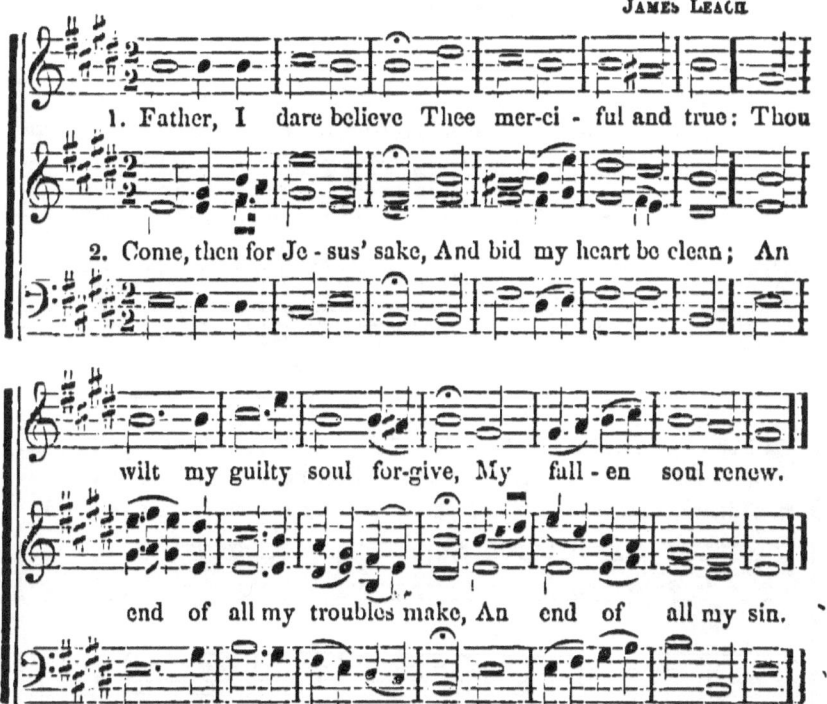

1. Father, I dare believe Thee mer-ci-ful and true: Thou wilt my guilty soul for-give, My fall-en soul renew.

2. Come, then for Je-sus' sake, And bid my heart be clean; An end of all my troubles make, An end of all my sin.

3 I cannot wash my heart,
But by believing thee,
And waiting for thy blood to' impart
The spotless purity.

4 While at thy cross I lie,
Jesus, the grace bestow;
Now thy all-cleansing blood apply,
And I am white as snow.

Conclusion of hymn on opposite page.

4 A home in heaven! when the faint heart bleeds,
By the Spirit's stroke, for its evil deeds;
O, then what bliss in that heart forgiven
Does the hope inspire of a home in heaven.

5 A home in heaven! when our friends are fled
To the cheerless gloom of the mouldering dead;
We wait in hope on the promise given;
We will meet up there in our home in heaven.

6 Our home in heaven! O, the glorious home,
And the Spirit, joined with the bride, says "Come!"
Come, seek his face, and your sins forgiven,
And rejoice in hope of your home in heaven

SHINING SHORE. 8s & 7s.

From "Sabbath Bell," by permission. G. F. Root.

1. My days are gliding swiftly by, And I, a pilgrim stranger, Would not detain them as they fly,—Those hours of toil and danger.

D. S. just before, the shining shore We may almost dis-cov-er.

CHORUS. For O, we stand on Jordan's strand, Our friends are passing over, And

2 We'll gird our loins, my brethren dear,
  Our distant home discerning;
  Our absent Lord has left us word,
  Let every lamp be burning.

3 Should coming days be cold and dark,
  We need not cease our singing;
  That perfect rest naught can molest,
  Where golden harps are ringing.

4 Let sorrow's rudest tempests blow,
  Each chord on earth to sever,
  Our King says come, and there's our home.
  Forever! O, forever!

WILMOT. 7s

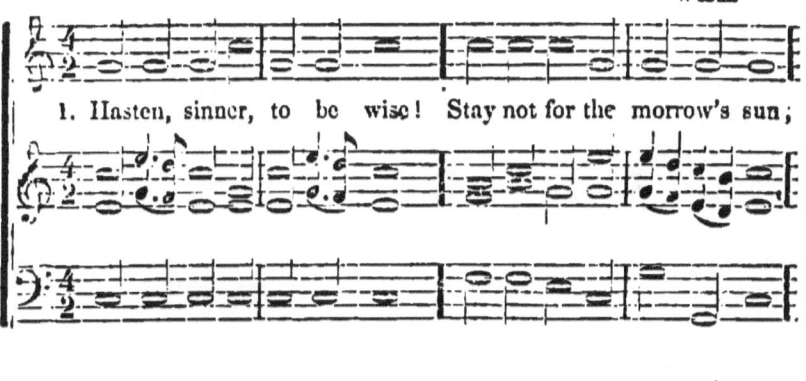

2 Hasten, mercy to implore!
  Stay not for the morrow's sun,
  Lest thy season should be o'er
  Ere this evening's stage be run.

3 Hasten, sinner, to return!
  Stay not for the morrow's sun,
  Lest thy lamp should fail to burn
  Ere salvation's work is done.

4 Hasten, sinner, to be blest!
  Stay not for the morrow's sun,
  Lest perdition thee arrest
  Ere the morrow is begun.

For a general blessing.

1 Lord, we come before thee now,
  At thy feet we humbly bow;
  O, do not our suit disdain;
  Shall we seek thee, Lord, in vain?

2 Lord, on thee our souls depend;
  In compassion now descend;
  Fill our hearts with thy rich grace,
  Tune our lips to sing thy praise.

3 Send some message from thy word,
  That may joy and peace afford;
  Let thy spirit now impart
  Full salvation to each heart.

4 Comfort those who weep and mourn;
  Let the time of joy return;
  Those that are cast down, lift up;
  Make them strong in faith and hope.

5 Grant that all may seek and find
  Thee, a gracious God and kind:
  Heal the sick, the captive free:
  Let us all rejoice in thee.

TAPPAN. 8s & 6s. 183

GEO. KINGSLEY, by permission.

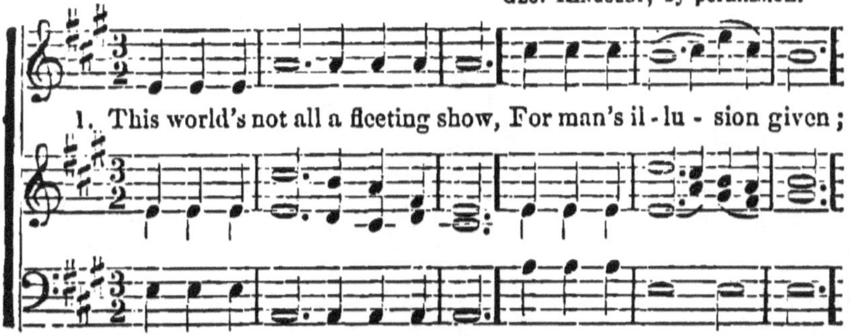

1. This world's not all a fleeting show, For man's il-lu-sion given;
He that hath soothed a widow's wo, Or wiped an orphan's tear, doth know
There's something here of heav'n.

2 And he that walks life's thorny way,
With feelings calm and even,—
Whose path is lit from day to day
By virtue's bright and steady ray,
Hath something felt of heaven.

3 He that the Christian's course has run
And all his foes forgiven,
Who measures out life's little span
In love to God and love to man,
On earth has tasted heaven.

Conclusion of hymn on opposite page.

2 That land is called the City of Light;
It ne'er has known the shades of night;
For the glory of God as the light of day,
Hath driven the darkness far away.

3 In vision I see its streets of gold,
Its gates of pearl I too behold,—
The river of life, the crystal sea,
The ambrosial fruit of life's fair tree.

4 That beautiful land I mean to see,
And join in its glorious harmony;
On the mount of God thro' grace I'll stand
And share in the bliss of that beautiful land.
J. HALL.

SONG OF VICTORY. C. M.

Music by REV. L. HARTSOUGH.

1. Je-ru-salem, my happy home, O how I long for thee;
When will my sorrows have an end, Thy joys, when shall I see?
Thy walls are all of precious stones, Most glorious to behold;
Thy gates are richly set with pearl, Thy streets are paved with gold.

2 Thy gardens and thy pleasant walks,
  My study long have been;
Such dazzling views, by human sight
  Have never yet been seen.
If Heav'n be thus so glorious, Lord,
  Why should I stay from hence?
What folly's this, that I should dread
  To die, and go from hence?

3 Reach down, O Lord, thine arm of grace
  And cause me to ascend,
Where congregations ne'er break up,
  And Sabbaths never end.

Jesus, my Lord, to glory's gone,
  Him will I go and see,
And all my brethren here below,
  Will soon come after me.

4 My friends, I bid you all adieu,
  I leave you in God's care;
And if I never see you,
  Go on, I'll meet you there.
When we've been there ten thousand years
  Bright shining as the sun,
We've no less days to sing God's praise,
  Than when we first begun.

WOODSTOCK. C. M. 185

D. DUTTON, JUN.

1. I love to steal awhile away From every cumb'ring care, And spend the hours of setting day In humble, grateful prayer.

2 I love in solitude to shed
  The penitential tear,
And all his promises to plead,
  Where none but God can hear.

3 I love to think on mercies past,
  And future good implore,—
And all my cares and sorrows cast
  On Him whom I adore.

4 I love by faith to take a view
  Of brighter scenes in heaven;
The prospect doth my strength renew,
  While here by tempests driven.

5 Thus, when life's toilsome day is o'er,
  May its departing ray
Be calm as this impressive hour,
  And lead to endless day.

Excellency and sufficiency.

1 Father of mercies, in thy word
  What endless glory shines;
Forever be thy Name adored
  For these celestial lines.

2 Here may the wretched sons of want
  Exhaustless riches find;
Riches above what earth can grant,
  And lasting as the mind.

3 Here the fair tree of knowledge grows,
  And yields a free repast;
Sublimer sweets than nature knows
  Invite the longing taste.

4 Here the Redeemer's welcome voice
  Spreads heavenly peace around;
And life, and everlasting joys,
  Attend the blissful sound.

5 O may these heavenly pages be
  Our ever dear delight;
And still new beauties may we see,
  And still increasing light.

6 Divine Instructer, gracious Lord,
  Be thou forever near;
Teach us to love thy sacred word,
  And view the Saviour there.

DUKE STREET. L. M.

JOHN HATTON.

1. From every stormy wind that blows, From every swelling tide of woes,

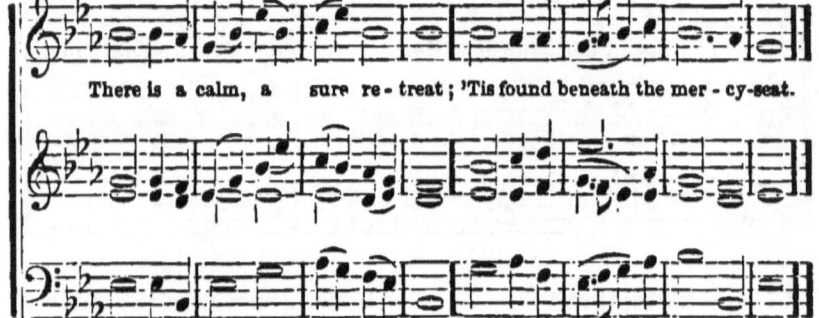

There is a calm, a sure re-treat; 'Tis found beneath the mer-cy-seat.

The mercy-seat.

2 There is a place, where Jesus sheds
The oil of gladness on our heads;
A place than all besides more sweet,—
It is the blood-bought mercy-seat.

3 There is a scene, where spirits blend,
Where friend holds fellowship with friend;
Though sundered far, by faith they meet,
Around one common mercy-seat.

4 Ah! whither could we flee for aid,
When tempted, desolate, dismayed?
Or how the hosts of hell defeat,
Had suffering saints no mercy-seat?

5 There, there on eagles' wings we soar,
And sin and sense molest no more;
And heav'n comes down our souls to greet,
While glory crowns the mercy-seat.

For lowliness and purity.

1 Jesus, in whom the Godhead's rays
Beam forth with mildest majesty;
I see thee full of truth and grace,
And come for all I want to thee.

2 Save me from pride,—the plague expel;
Jesus, thine humble self impart:
O let thy mind within me dwell;
O give me lowliness of heart.

3 Enter thyself, and cast out sin;
Thy spotless purity bestow:
Touch me, and make the leper clean;
Wash me, and I am white as snow.

4 Sprinkle me, Saviour, with thy blood,
And all thy gentleness is mine;
And plunge me in the purple flood,
Till all I am is lost in thine.

CORONATION. C. M.

OLIVER HOLDEN.

1. All hail the power of Jesus' name, Let angels prostrate fall; Bring forth the royal di-a-dem, And crown him Lord of all, Bring forth the royal di-a-dem, And crown him Lord of all.

Coronation of Christ.

2 Ye chosen seed of Israel's race,
  Ye ransomed from the fall,
  Hail him, who saves you by his grace,
  And crown him Lord of all

3 Let every kindred, every tribe,
  On this terrestrial ball,
  To him all majesty ascribe,
  And crown him Lord of all.

4 O that with yonder sacred throng,
  We at his feet may fall;
  We'll join the everlasting song,
  And crown him Lord of all.

INDEX OF TUNES AND METRES.

Tune	Metre	Page
A beautiful home for thee	P. M.	33
A closer walk with God	C. M.	78
A home in Heaven	P. M.	178
Alas! and did my Saviour	C. M.	27
Amsterdam	7s & 6s.	100
America	6s & 4s.	148
Angels bear me away	C. M.	134
Angels guarding me	8s & 7s.	10
Angels round me	8s & 7s.	37
Arlington	C. M.	155
Atonement	P. M.	119
Azmon	C. M.	110
Balerma	C. M.	171
Bethlehem	8s & 7s.	160
Beautiful Zion	8s.	101
Boylston	S. M.	116
Bridgewater	L. M.	117
Cambridge	C. M.	128
China	C. M.	127
Christ our Pilot	8s & 7s.	49
Cleansing Fountain	C. M.	13
Consolation	C. M.	24
Concord	S. M	157
Conway	C. M.	73
Come ye disconsolate	11s & 10s.	83
Cowper	C. M.	107
Coronation	C. M.	187
Cross and Crown	C. M.	132
Depth of Mercy	7s.	151
Dedham	C. M.	88
Did Christ o'er sinners weep?	S.M.	62
Down by the River	P. M.	8
Dundee	C. M.	103
Duke Street	L. M.	186
Elizabethtown	C. M.	136
Emmons	C. M.	130
Evening	7s.	39
Expostulation	11s.	169
Exhortation	C. M.	170
Forever with the Lord	S. M.	82
Ganges	C. P. M.	111
Glory to the Lamb	P. M.	163
Going Home	P. M.	53
God is near thee	6s & 5s.	21
God is Love	L. M.	5
God is everywhere	7s.	54
Haddam	H. M.	71
Hamburg	L. M.	147
Happy Day	L. M.	105
He is precious	7s & 6s.	16
Heber	C. M.	69
Hebron	L. M.	106
Here is no rest	P. M.	97
Heaven's not far away	C. M.	18
Hendon	7s.	141
Home of the blest	11s	30
Homeward bound	P. M.	135
Home at last	P. M.	86
Horton	6 lines 7s.	137
I long to be there	P. M.	41
I love Thee	11s.	165
I'm going Home	L. M.	144
I'm a traveller	7s & 4s.	158
Immanuel's Birth	P. M.	34
I soon shall see the day	C. M.	32
Italian Hymn	6s & 4s	149
I will not let thee go	6 lines, 8s.	43
Jesus calls you	P. M.	7
Jesus paid it all	P. M.	55
Journeying home to Heaven	P. M.	64
Joyfully	P. M.	72
Joyful sound	C. M.	91
Just as I am	8s.	159
Lake Enon	S. M.	9
Let go the Anchor	8s & 7s.	31
Lenox	H. M.	123
Lift me higher	8s & 7s.	44
Light is breaking	8s & 7s.	17
Lisbon	S. M.	113
Lyons	10s & 11s.	145
Mason	L. M.	153
Man the Life-boat	8s & 7s.	92
Majesty	C. M.	166
Martyn	7s.	79

INDEX OF TUNES AND METRES.

Mercy's free ....P. M. 38
Meribah ....C. P. M. 150
Mendon ....L. M. 151
Mear ....C. M. 146
My Fatherland.............P. M. 156

Nashville. ....L. P. M. 142
Nearer, my God, to Thee. ...P. M. 45
Nettleton..................8s & 7s. 139
Newton 8s. 95
New Jerusalem ....C. M. 167
Northfield. ....C. M. 143
No parting There ....S. M. 93
No-night in Heaven..........10s. 174
Nuremburg....................7s. 90

Oh, I want to cross over....P. M. 40
Old Hundred................L. M. 67
Olmutz ....S. M. 131
On the Cross ....P. M. 152
Onward and upward ....P. M. 59
Our loved ones in Heaven...P. M. 48
Our Soldier Boy is missing. P. M. 61
Ortonville..................C. M. 140
O sing to me of Heaven....S. M. 98
O where shall rest be found.S. M. 19

Peterborough...............C. M. 81
Pilgrim Song...............P. M. 162
Pleading Saviour........8s. & 7s. 175
Pleyel's Hymn................7s 15
Port of Glory.............8s & 7s. 58

Rest for the weary.........P. M. 138
Rest.........................L. M. 133
Repentance ....P. M. 36
Rockingham ....L. M. 112

Sabbath Morn 7s. 120
Saint's Coronation day .....L. M. 11
Salvation ....C. M. 20
Seraphic Fire..........4 lines 7s. 12
Shining Shore ....8s & 7s. 180
Shirland ....S. M 91
Shall we meet? ....8s & 7s. 66
Shall we know each other? .P. M. 22
Silver Street ....S. M. 161
Sinner's Invitation ....6s & 7s. 80
Siloam.....................C. M. 68

Sicily......................8s & 7s. 109
St. Thomas...................S. M. 177
St. Martin's................C. M. 89
Sunny Side................8s & 7s. 76
Sweet rest in Heaven.......P. M. 164
Sweet hour of Prayer ......L. M. 63

Tappan...................8s & 6s. 183
That beautiful River........P. M. 51
They are waiting for me..8s & 7s. 46
Then roll, roll away ....P. M. 57
There, there is rest..........P. M. 23
The bleeding Saviour ......C. M. 87
The City of Light..........P. M. 183
The Christian Hero ....P. M. 56
The Eden above..........12s & 11s. 108
The Lion of Judah.........P. M. 14
The language of the Cross..C. M. 4
The Saviour's invitation....C. M. 102
The tomb is void............6s. 3
The Union Band............P. M. 50
The wanderer recalled......L. M. 6
The year of release .... .P. M. 53
To my mother in Heaven...C. M. 176
Turner.....................C. M. 108

Uxbridge...................L. M. 118

Victory....................P. M. 124

Watchman...................S. M. 179
Watchman, tell us of the.4 lines 7s. 172
Ware ....L. M. 74
Ward........................L. M. 104
Waiting for the Boatman.8s & 7s. 60
Webb ....7s & 6s. 84
Wells ....L. M. 129
Welton.....................L. M, 114
What shall I do to be saved? P.M. 65
Who can tell?..................8s. 25
Why not go?...............8s & 6s. 47
Wilmot......................7s. 181
Willie's gone before........C. M. 26
Will you be there? ......C. P. M. 42
Woodstock ....C. M. 185
Woodland ....C. M. 115
Wrestling Jacob.........6 lines 8s. 28

Zephyr ....L. M. 121
Zion's Pilgrim ....L. M. 29

INDEX OF HYMNS.

	Page.
A beautiful land by faith I see...	182
A home in heaven! what a	178
Alas, and did my Saviour bleed 27,	87
All hail! happy day............	34
All hail the power of Jesus' name	187
Almighty Maker, God	94
Almighty Spirit, now behold	136
Am I a soldier of the Cross	155
And may I still get there	93
And can I yet delay.	113
And am I only born to die.	150
Are you waiting, angel mother...	46
Arise, my soul, arise.............	123
Auspicious morning, hail........	148
Awake, my soul! stretch every ..	144
Behold, behold the Lamb of.....	152
Behold the Saviour of mankind..	87
Behold the throne of grace	94
Beautiful Zion, built above	101
Beyond this life of hopes and....	42
Blest be the dear uniting love....	110
Blessed angels are around me....	10
Blessed Jesus, when I see........	36
Breast the wave, Christian.......	59
By faith I see my Saviour dying..	38
By cool Siloam's shady rill	68
Come, thou fount of every blessing	139
Come ye that love the Lord......	157
Come sound his praise abroad....	161
Come thou everlasting Spirit	161
Come, let us join our cheerful....	73
Come, O thou traveller unkn'n.	28, 43
Come, poor pilgrims, sad and....	23
Come, all ye saints, to Pisgah....	48
Come, ye disconsolate	83
Come, humble sinner..........	13, 107
Come Holy Spirit, heavenly	108
Come on my partners	111
Come, weary sinners, come......	113
Come, my soul, thy suit.	141
Come, thou Almighty King......	149
Come, Holy Ghost, our hearts....	136
Come brethren, don't grow	164

	Page.
Daughter of Zion, from the dust.	129
Day of God, thou blessed day ...	141
Depth of mercy! can there be...	151
Delightful work! young souls....	81
Did Christ o'er sinners weep ..62,	94
Father of mercies in thy word,..	185
Father, I dare believe............	179
Forever with the Lord...........	82
Forever here my rest	89
From the third heavens..........	167
From Greenland's icy	173
From the Cross uplifted..........	99
From every stormy wind	186
Glorious things of thee are	160
God is in the torrent's fall	54
Grace! 'tis a charming sound....	98
Great God, attend while.	117
Great God, indulge..............	118
Happy the spirit released........	124
Hasten sinner to be wise	181
Happy the man who finds.	106
He's gone to that fair land.	26
Here o'er the earth as a.........	97
How helpless nature lies	131
How blest the sacred tie.........	133
How vain is all beneath..........	133
How tedious and tasteless........	95
How sweetly flowed	104
How happy is the pilgrim's lot.47,	111
Home at last....	86
How vain are all things..........	146
How sweet the hour of	147
I am standing down by death's ..	8
I cannot always trace thy way. ..	5
If thou impart thyself.	115
I heard the voice of Jesus say. ..	102
I love to steal awhile away.......	185
I love Thee.....................	165
I love thy kingdom, Lord........	177
I'm looking for Jesus............	57
I'm very near my Father's house.	18

INDEX OF HYMNS.

I'm a lonely traveller	158
In the Christian's home	138
In our household band	61
In evil long I took delight	4
In heaven, bright heaven	30
I saw one hanging on a tree	27
I thirst, thou wounded Lamb	118
Jesus, the sinner's friend	74
Jesus, lover of my soul	173
Jesus, great Shepherd of	103
Jesus, in whom the	186
Joyfully, joyfully	72
Just as I am, without	150
Land ahead! its fruits	31
Let every tongue thy goodness	132
Listen to the whisperings	21
Lift me higher	44
Live on the field of battle	56
Light of life, seraphic fire	12
Life is the time to serve	129
Lo! the gospel ship is sailing	58
Lord, we come before thee now	181
Lord, dismiss us	109
Look unto Christ, ye nations	110
Lord, how secure and blest	112
Lovers of pleasure more than	115
Man the life boat	92
Majestic sweetness sits	140
Mary to the Saviour's tomb	79
Must Jesus bear the cross	132
My country, 'tis of thee	148
My days are gliding	180
My former hopes are fled	116
My heavenly home is bright	144
My hope, my all	153
My latest sun is sinking	134
My soul is now united	16
Nearer, my God, to Thee	45
Nought of merit, or of price	55
No night shall be in heaven	174
Now the Saviour stands, and	175
O aged believer, whose feet	53
Of him who did salvation	106
O for a thousand tongues	143
O for a faith that will not	60
O for a glance of heavenly	74
O for a closer walk with	140
O for a heart to praise my	89
O God, our help in ages	146

O how divine, how sweet	171
O how happy are they	35
O happy day that fixed	105
O have you not heard	51
O have you not heard of that	40
O joyful sound of gospel	91
O Jesus full of truth	142
O Lord thy work revive	131
On Jordan's stormy banks	170
Once more, my soul, the rising	81
Once I thought my mountain	99
O sing to me of heaven	98
O that I could repent	62
O that my load of sin	104
O thou who dryest	69
O thou from whom all	132
O turn ye	169
Our Canaan fair	47
Out on an ocean	135
O we're a band of brethren	50
O what shall I do to	65
O where shall rest be found	19
Pilgrims we are to Canaan	29
Praise God from whom	67
Praise waits in Zion	154
Prayer is appointed to convey	112
Return, O wandering soul	6
Return, O wanderer, return	114
Rise, my soul, and stretch	100
Rock of ages, cleft for me	157
Sailor, enter not life's voyage	49
Salvation, O the joyful sound	20
Safely through another week	120
Saviour, I now with shame	129
Saw ye my Saviour	119
Servant of God, in joyful	154
See, Jesus, thy disciples see	89
Shall we meet beyond the river	66
Sinners turn while God	12
Sinners, we are sent to bid	7
Sinner go, will you go	80
Sing praise! the tomb is void	3
Sow in the morn thy seed	116
Softly now the light of day	39
Softly fades the twilight	15
Stay thou insulted Spirit	6
Sweet hour of prayer	63
Sweet day of rest	11
Sweet was the time when	88
Sweet the moments, rich	76

There's a beautiful home for thee.	33
There are angels hovering round.	37
There is a fountain filled	13
There is a place when my	156
The flowery fields of youth	25
The hill of Zion yields	157
The world is overcome	163
The night comes stealing on	176
The Lord Jehovah reigns	71
The morning light is breaking.	84
The Lord descended from	166
This world's not all a	183
This is the day the Lord.	107
Thou dear Redeemer	130
Though troubles assail	145
Thou Lamb of God	114
Thou hidden source	142
Thus fear the Lord	147
Through a strange country	52
'Twas Jesus, my Saviour	14
Vain man, thy fond	127
Watchman, tell me, does the	17
Watchman, tell us of the	172
Walk in the light	155
We are watching by the river	60
We are journeying home to	64
We're bound for the land	168
Weary souls that wander	137
When we hear the music.	22
When languor and disease	24
When I think of that city.	41
When I can read my title clear	32
While my Redeemer's near	9
Whither, pilgrim, are you going	162
Why do we mourn	127
Why should our tears.	68
Why should we start	121
Why should the children	171

www.ingramcontent.com/pod-product-compliance
Lightning Source LLC
Chambersburg PA
CBHW032138160426
43197CB00008B/691